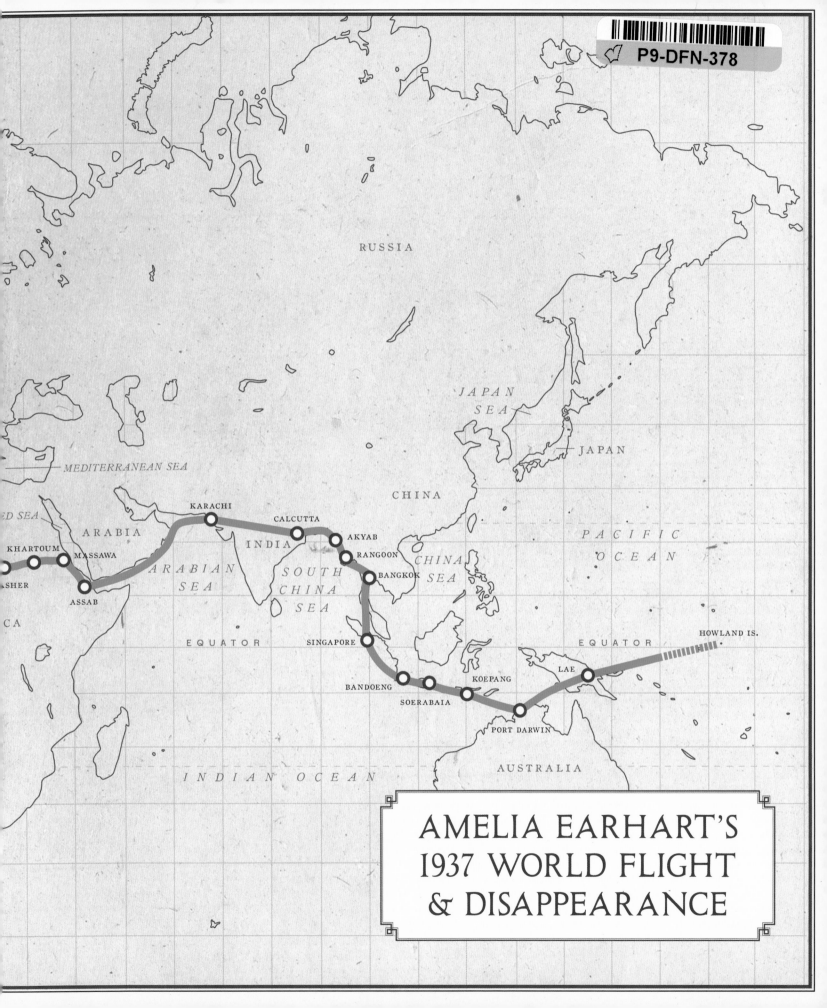

AMELIA EARHART'S 1937 WORLD FLIGHT & DISAPPEARANCE

AMELIA EARHART

the
thrill
of it

AMELIA EARHART

the **thrill** of it

SUSAN WELS

RUNNING PRESS
PHILADELPHIA • LONDON

Original poems quoted on p. 146 with permission of Purdue
University Libraries

Library of Congress Control Number: 2009926750

ISBN 978-0-7624-3763-4

Cover and interior design by Debbie Berne, Oakland, CA
www.debbiebernedesign.com

Edited by Jennifer Kasius

The book is set in FF Scala and ITC Franklin Gothic.
The display type is Roslyn.

Running Press Book Publishers
2300 Chestnut Street
Philadelphia, PA 19103-4371

Visit us on the web!
www.runningpress.com

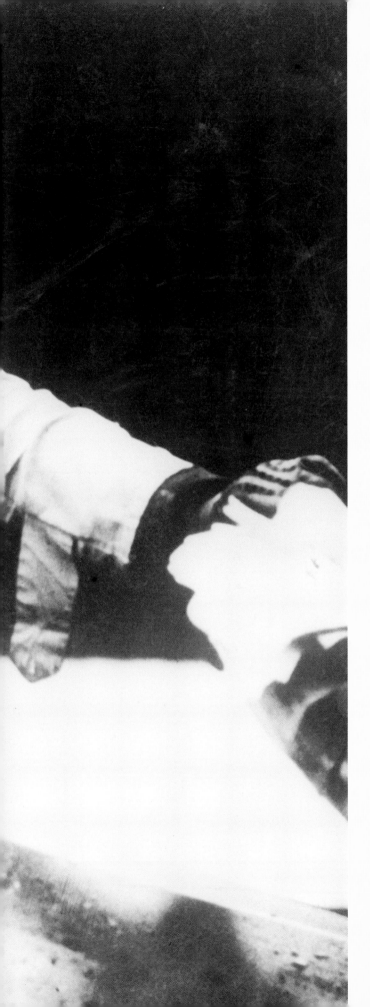

CONTENTS

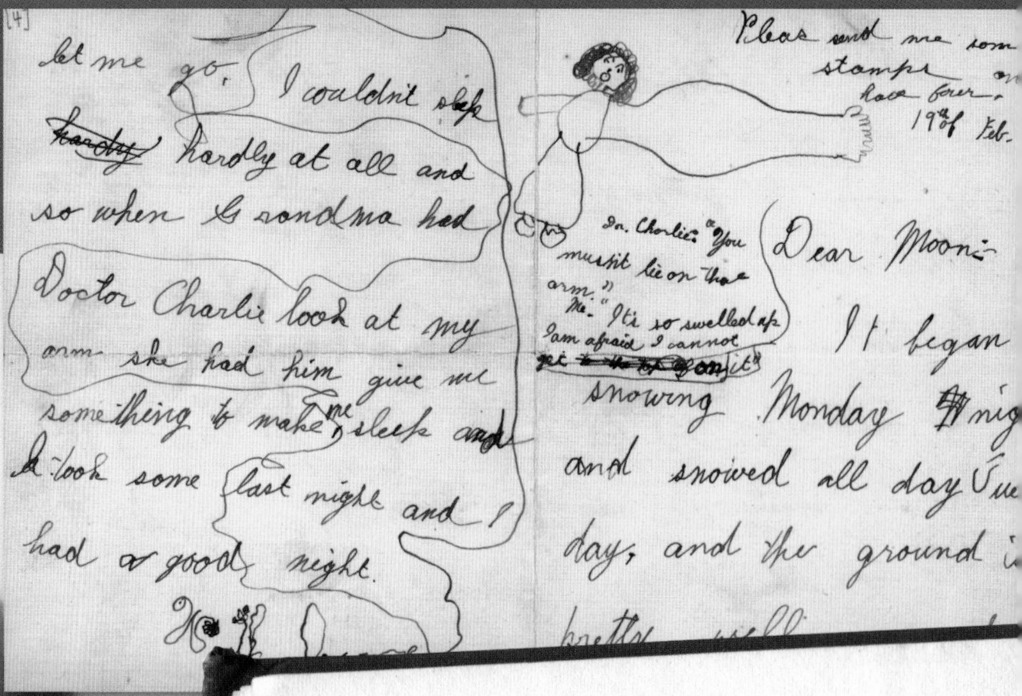

[4]

let me go. I couldn't sleep
~~hardly~~ hardly at all and
so when Grandma had
Doctor Charlie look at my
arm she had him give me
something to make me sleep and
I took some last night and I
had a good night.

Please send me some
stamps on
hace four—
19th of Feb.

Dr. Charlie: "You
mustn't lie on that
arm."
Me. "It is so swelled up
I am afraid I cannot
~~get it~~ ~~try~~ ~~on it~~ it."

Dear Moon—

It began
snowing Monday night
and snowed all day Tues-
day, and the ground is
pretty well covered

AMELIA EARHART

Miss Earhart.

Women Pilots all over the World are very proud of your magnificent achievement and the dig- nified way in which you have done it. I am personally looking forward [to] meeting you [congrat-] ulate you person[ally on your] wonderful galla[ntry]

Mary H[eath]

Aero Club of Oregon
PORTLAND CHAPTER, NATIONAL AERONAUTIC ASSN.
Membership Card
This is to Certify that *Amelia Earhart*
Aero Club of Oregon
IS AN HONORARY LIFE MEMBER
M. F. Wright
SECRETARY
Feb. 1-1933
DATE

SHEPHERD FIELD
ESTABLISHED 1922
Mrs Amelia Earhart Putnam
IS A MEMBER OF THE
[BER]KELEY AVIATION CLUB
MARTINSBURG, WEST VIRGINIA
HIGHLY COMMENDED BY
[U.]S. ARMY AIR CORPS. U.S. MARINE CORPS
[U.]S. NAVY, BUREAU OF AERONAUTICS
NATIONAL AERONAUTIC ASSOCIATION
Alex B. Parks
SECRETARY
REGULA[R]
IN GOOD STANDING OF THE
[Nation]al Aeronautical Association of U.S.A.
(INCORPORATED)
MEMBERSHIP EXPIRES APRIL 1. 1933
M B Peabody
SECRETARY

a E Book

THRILL

recent
On my flight from Hawaii, I had been so busy with my
motor, fuel supply, instruments and radio that I had given no
_____ round me. When the moon set, there
_____ e night. The horizon was so low
_____ eath me! I knew it was an illusion,
_____ eering over the edge of the black
_____ from below. All of my life there
_____ ere stars beneath! Beauty and
_____ not cry it aloud. There were no
_____ e vibrant, icy, numbing waves
_____ soul to mind, "I know. I know."
_____ thrilling, to describe trivial
_____ e only a few things are thrilling
_____ s with sudden awareness of
_____ e trembles with the discovery.
_____ ation, to the light that
_____ sudden consciousness of hidden
_____ and the freedom of self.
_____ over all protest and in spite
of all adversity, I sometimes thrill, not with the task but with
the realization that I am doing what I want to do

PREFACE

Everyone knows the name Amelia Earhart, but few know the colorful, fascinating, and much-photographed personality behind the legend. It wasn't until a good friend spoke to me about her, out of the blue, that I realized how little I knew about Amelia Earhart. And the more I learned, the more amazed I was at the character, complexity, accomplishments, and raw courage of this singular woman.

She was the most famous woman in America, and she was ahead of her time. Born in 1897, Amelia defied convention and loved doing it; she was driven, self-directed, and unafraid. "When I undertake a task over all protest and in spite of all adversity, I sometimes thrill," she wrote, with "the realization that I am doing what I want to do." Professionally, she constantly crossed boundaries, and in her personal life, too, she refused limits. When she married publisher and publicist George Palmer (G. P.) Putnam in 1931, she rejected the "medieval code of faithfulness" and "the confinements of even an attractive cage."

In June 1937, Amelia took off on a round-the-world flight at the equator, the first person ever to attempt to do so. When people asked her why, she replied, "because I want to." She never shied away from a grand adventure; the dangers of the exploit, over two oceans and four continents, were no deterrence. When people warned her of the hazards of an undertaking, "I could scarcely wait," she responded, "to be on my way." A month after she set out—after crossing the Atlantic, South America, Africa, South Asia, and the South Pacific—Amelia vanished over the Pacific Ocean. No trace of her remains or plane has ever been found, and the circumstances of her disappearance are still a mystery.

Since the publication of Amelia's own books—*20 Hrs., 40 Mins.* in 1928, *The Fun of It* in 1932, and *Last Flight,* a posthumous narrative published in 1937—many authors have researched and chronicled her life. More recently, however, new information has come to light that adds richness, complexity, and emotional nuance to Amelia's story. In 1997, G. P.'s granddaughter, Sally Putnam Chapman, published a biography of her grandmother—G. P.'s first wife, Dorothy Putnam—based on her extraordinarily frank diary entries. This intimate new information provides fascinating insights into the relationship between Amelia and Dorothy, who were good friends, and their passions and shared attachments to G. P. I am grateful to Sally Putnam Chapman for these revelations and her generous assistance in the details of photo research.

Important new materials have also become available since 2002, when Purdue University Library's Archives and Special Collections acquired the George Palmer Putnam Collection of Amelia Earhart Papers. Donated by Sally Putnam Chapman, the collection includes a wealth of personal documents, including letters and love poetry, that deepen the interpretation of Amelia's life.

Seventy years after she was declared dead, the mystery of Amelia's disappearance is as compelling and confounding as it was in 1937. She is still America's most famous missing person, and this book updates the continuing search for clues in remote reaches of the South Pacific, thanks to the generous help of investigators David Jourdan and Ric Gillespie.

Amelia has always been an icon—not just in her time, but in ours—and her visual image made, and continues to make, as powerful an impression as her character and achievements. In the more than three hundred photographs and other images in this book, Amelia comes to life in a way that words can't duplicate. From the time she was a child, Amelia always stood out in the crowd. Her androgynous glamour and quiet courage were bigger than life, and she lived to the limit.

This biography would never have been possible without the help of many talented and patient individuals. My thanks to Jesse Kershner for the inspiration; my friend and literary agent, Carole Bidnick, who midwived and godmothered this book from the very beginning; the project's superbly gifted art director and designer, Debbie Berne; and the supportive and responsive team at Runnning Press, including editor Jennifer Kasius, Vice President and Associate Publisher Craig Herman, Publisher Christopher Navratil, and Design Director Bill Jones. Thanks, too, to Sheridan McCarthy and Laurie Dunne for their fine editorial services.

I spent days in the archives at the Purdue University Library and the Schlesinger Library at Harvard's Radcliffe Institute, and for months after, their staff members were unfailingly helpful. I would especially like to thank Carl Snow, Sammie Morris, Stephanie Schmitz, and Elizabeth Wilkinson at Purdue University Archives and Special Collections and Diana Carey and Sarah Hamberton at Radcliffe's Schlesinger Library at Harvard University. In addition, I am grateful to Louise Foudray at the Amelia Earhart Birthplace Museum, Bryan McDaniel at the Chicago History Museum; Judy Reale, Albert Rozo, and Sam Stormont at Pennsylvania State University; Jen Young at the British Red Cross Museum and Archives; Adam Garel-Frantzen at Getty Images; Kelsie Ede at Corbis; Kate Igoe and Melissa Keiser at the National Air and Space Museum; James O'Donnell at the National Postal Museum; Dorothy Cochrane at the Smithsonian; David Hegeman at Oregon State Library; Craig Morris; Wendy Glassmire at National Geographic Society; Bill Meixner in Cleveland, Ohio; Dr. Russell Naughton at Monash University in Melbourne; Carolyn Smith at the Ninety-Nines Museum of Women Pilots; Heather Taylor of *Rag Wing Derby;* John Waggener at the American Heritage Center; Ann Sindelar at Western Reserve Historical Society Library and Archives; Caryn Kanare at *Cosmopolitan* magazine; JoAnn Schwartz; Reid Dennis; John Wischmann; and Fred Patterson.

Thanks also to many friends for their unstinting support and guidance, including Liz Perle, Joan Kampe O'Connor, David Cohen, Jude Lange, Maggie Hallahan, Ronni Kass, Arin Fishkin, Mark Robertson, Barbara Ochsner, and Michael Phelan. Finally, my deepest thanks to family members for their encouragement and patience, especially David, Emily, and Casey Hagerman and David Murray.

the thrill of it

1

THE GIRL IN BROWN WHO WALKS ALONE

On a clear day in January 1921, a tall, slender young woman—wearing brown breeches, high laced boots, and a brown jacket—walked miles down a dusty highway to a weedy airfield surrounded by vegetable farms south of Los Angeles. Amelia Earhart—well groomed, with a library book on aerodynamics tucked under her arm—would have stood out in any crowd, according to her flying instructor. She was a loner—her high school yearbook dubbed her "the girl in brown who walks alone"—but she was also a leader, a bookish tomboy who was more fun and adventurous than anyone else and who threw herself at experience, especially the wildly exciting kind. She also had her inner "deeps," private wells of emotion and sharp sensitivities that she felt profoundly but seldom shared.

Opposite Amelia Mary Earhart at age seventeen

Below Her grand-parents, Amelia Harres Otis and Judge Alfred Otis

Amelia was born in the calm after a lightning storm on the night of July 24, 1897, in her grandparents' large home in Atchison, Kansas. Standing high on a bluff over the Missouri River, it was the home where her mother, Amy, had grown up and returned to give birth at her parents' urging. Amy's father, Alfred Otis, was a bank president and retired judge of the United States District Court. An ardent abolitionist, he had come to Kansas in 1855 to help escaping slaves— hiding them in trunks and covering them with grain in the backs of wagons—and to bring Kansas into the Union as a free state. By the 1890s, he had made a fortune in land speculation and a profitable law practice and was one of the growing commercial town's reigning citizens.

Amelia's parents, Amy Otis and Edwin Stanton Earhart, on their wedding day in 1895

of Atchison's young social set and the belles of local cotillions and military balls. An excellent student and fine rider, Amy had hoped to attend Vassar in 1889, but she caught diptheria and abandoned her plans due to a long convalescence and her parents' reluctance to send her to college so far from Kansas.

Instead, Amy's life took a different turn. That year, at her coming-out party, she met Edwin Earhart and decided that they "danced very well together." Edwin, the son of a scholarly Lutheran minister, was brilliant and good-looking but relatively poor. He had shined shoes, tended furnaces, and performed other menial work to pay his way through Kansas University, and he and his family lived in "sore straits" outside of town. Captivated by spirited, chestnut-haired Amy Otis, he was no doubt also impressed by her family's material comforts and social standing. The couple courted and planned to marry, but Judge Otis refused to consent until Edwin was able to earn at least $50 a month, a considerable sum, to support his bride. It was five years before Edwin was able to meet that challenge through a job as a claims attorney for a railroad. In October 1895, he and Amy married at last and left Atchison by train for Kansas City, Missouri, where they moved into their wedding present from the judge, a small home he had purchased and completely furnished for them on Ann Avenue.

He and his wife, Amelia, raised Amy, like her sister and four brothers, to "love the smell of a book" and the joy of adventure. The family read and traveled widely, by stagecoach and carriage, through the newly settled states and territories of the West, including Utah, Oklahoma, Colorado, and California. Judge Otis, Amy later recalled, wanted his family "to have seeing eyes," to embrace new experiences, and to keep them in memory. In their spacious, book-filled home on Quality Hill, the Otis children grew up steeped in music, literature, history, art, mathematics, foreign languages, and worldly discussions with friends and neighbors like Senator John Ingalls and Governor John Martin. Amy and Constance Ingalls, the senator's daughter, were the leaders

The first year of marriage was hard for Amy, who loved her husband but not always her life as the housekeeping wife of a struggling lawyer. Amy also suffered a traumatic miscarriage in the seventh month of her pregnancy that year, after a streetcar she was riding jerked and threw her violently against the brake lever. In the winter of 1896, when Amy discovered she was pregnant again, her parents persuaded her to come back to Atchison to

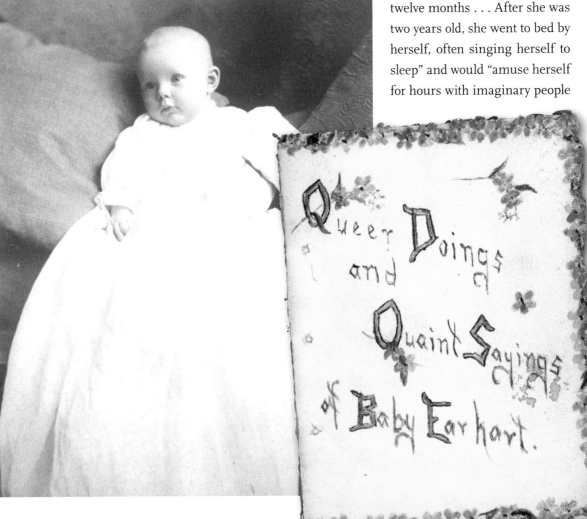

give birth in the family home, where she and her baby would be well looked after.

Amelia Mary Earhart, named after both her grandmothers, arrived in the world "tall with a beautifully shaped head and hands, a real water color baby with the bluest of blue eyes, rosy cheeks and red lips," her mother recorded in her handmade baby book, *Queer Doings and Quaint Sayings of Baby Earhart*. At nine pounds, her mother wrote,

"Millie" was perfectly proportioned; her weight "was not due to excess fat for her bones were small and nicely covered." From the start, Amelia was healthy and self-sufficient. She "talked to herself in the looking glass at the age of twelve months . . . After she was two years old, she went to bed by herself, often singing herself to sleep" and would "amuse herself for hours with imaginary people and playthings." Once, Amy overheard the child talking to herself; when Amelia discovered that her mother was in the room, she explained, "If you are not here to talk to, I just whisper in my own ears."

When a second daughter, Grace Muriel Earhart, was born in December 1899, Amy, whose

Left A baby book that Amy Earhart made for her first daughter, Amelia

Above Amelia Earhart at four months of age

Five-year-old Amelia with her little sister, Muriel, on their front porch in Kansas City

hands were full in Kansas City, decided to send Amelia fifty miles away to Atchison to live with her grandparents for a time. It was no hardship for Amelia, who grew to feel thoroughly at home in the big house on Quality Hill. It was also a welcome distraction for her grandmother, who was grieving the recent deaths of her mother, eldest son, and daughter-in-law. Amelia stayed in Atchison on and off throughout her grade-school years, enrolling in the same college preparatory school that her mother had attended. Amy and Muriel traveled

to Atchison frequently, the whole family celebrated holidays and birthdays together, and Amelia spent summers in Kansas City. In both family homes, Amelia and Muriel, who joined her sister in Atchison for a year, had a childhood that was almost idyllically playful and free from traditional constraints.

The girls—who called each other "Meelie" and "Pidge"—were "comfortable, unconventional, and entirely happy tomboys," Muriel remembered. They liked to play cowboys and Indians, hunter, and

Left Amelia (foreground) and Muriel—known as "Meelie" and "Pidge"—were unconventional and happy tomboys who loved baseball, football, mud-ball, and basketball.

Below Amelia (far left) with basketball and friends, between 1908 and 1912

made-up adventure games like "Bogie" and "The Pursuit of the Hairy Men"—climbing into an old carriage in the barn and taking exotic imaginary journeys, firing make-believe pistols at their pursuers. Their days were filled with baseball, football, mud-ball fights, and expeditions to explore sandstone caves and collect insects, spiders, skulls, and other specimens. Although their grandmother frowned on their boyish antics—Amelia Otis had never done anything more strenuous as a child, she told them, than roll a hoop—their mother rarely discouraged their adventures. Amy, it seems, had unlimited visions for her daughters.

When they were infants, she inscribed their baby book with a quote from Ruskin: "Shakespeare has no heroes; he has only heroines." She even freed them from the feminine restraints

of skirts, making them the first gymnasium suits in town, of dark blue flannel with pleated bloomers. "We wore them on Saturdays to play in," Amelia remembered, and

"felt terribly 'free and athletic,'" if a bit snubbed by the little girls who "fluttered about us in their skirts."

Edwin, too, was happy to have his daughters act "as much like boys" as they wanted. He played Chief in their Saturday cowboy and Indian battles, told them thrilling Western yarns that "ran on for weeks," and gave them long boys' sleds for Christmas, which they could ride bellyflopping down snowy hills, instead of short girls' sleds that were ridden in a prim position, sitting up. He also gave them footballs and a .22-caliber Hamilton

rifle, which they used for shooting rats in the old barn, a fascinating and compelling hobby for Amelia. She "gets an idea and, by gosh, she stays right with it," her grandparents' handyman observed. "Dinner or no dinner," he said, "punishment or not, she wanted to get the rats."

Amelia's persistence, however, occasionally went too far in her mother's eyes. Inspired by a trip to the 1904 World's Fair in St. Louis, where she was allowed to ride an elephant and the Ferris Wheel but not the high-speed roller coaster that went shrieking by, seven-year-old Amelia decided to build her own homemade roller coaster in Kansas City. Using two-by-fours and a wooden packing crate, she, Muriel, and their cousin Ralphie hammered and sawed together a rickety track that launched from the roof of the backyard tool shed. After greasing the track with half a bucket of lard, Amelia climbed into the crate, which she used as the coaster car, and took off with a yell, sliding down the track much faster than expected until she and the crate slammed into the ground. Despite her bruises and a torn dress, Amelia was thrilled—it was "just like flying," she exclaimed. Her mother had a different view of the exploit, which she considered dangerous, and had the makeshift roller coaster taken down.

Not all of Amelia's adventures, however, were physical in nature. She took "intense pleasure" in activity and sports, but she also played with imaginary friends and loved the smell of a book, just like her mother. She and Muriel both learned to read before they were five years old, and at an early age Amelia plunged into the world of literature. Instead of reading simple stories, which she considered childish, she would bury herself for hours in volumes by Scott, Dickens, George Eliot, and Thackeray, as well as countless issues of *Harper's Magazine for Young People* and *The Youth's Companion*. The Otis family in Atchison had always read together, and Amy, in turn, read to her daughters—a habit, Amelia recalled, that became "so fundamental" that when she and Muriel did housework together, one would work while the other read aloud.

Amelia's reading material wasn't all grown up and serious. She also loved comic strips, especially "The Katzenjammer Kids" with its funny, phonetic spelling of English words. Amelia made the trope her own, peppering her writing and letters with deliberate misspellings just for fun. Words in general had unusual significance for Amelia. She was sensitive to their sound and "music," her mother wrote, and would refuse to speak certain words because they sounded "harsh and disagreeable" and "hurt her ears." Amelia adored her father—the first word she ever uttered was "Papa"—and he shared her playful fascination with language. "I thought that my father must have read everything and, of course, therefore, knew everything," Amelia wrote. "He could define the hardest words as well as the dictionary" and once sent her a letter that began, "Dear parallelepipedon," which immediately sent her hunting for a definition.

Amelia's love for words drew her to poetry, although she seldom exhibited special talent as a writer. She wrote her first poem when she was between four and five years old, but "there was nothing striking about it," her mother noted. As Amelia grew up, writing became an outlet for her thoughts and feelings. "She was quite particular about words," Amy observed, but it was more about "the way she thought" and "liked to put things" than it was about literary style.

Looking back, Amelia remembered "having a very good time" throughout her grade school years, spent mainly in Atchison. She and Muriel especially loved the warmth and security of the Otis home. It was a feeling they often associated with the sound of their grandfather's heavy, black, handmade shoes that creaked when he crossed a room or rocked on his heels as he stood with his back to the fireplace.

Amelia, age ten, loved reading, playing cowboys and Indians, and shooting rats in the barn.

Below Edwin Earhart, a railroad attorney, often brought his family along on trips, believing that travel was more beneficial than formal schooling.

Bottom Amelia and Muriel pose with Edwin on a luxurious private railroad car—staffed by Tokimo (far right), a Japanese porter and cook—that the Rock Island line allowed them to use.

The sisters talked of their home "creaking with plenty," a feeling of pleasure and freedom they never forgot. Their companions from those years, for their part, never forgot Amelia. "Millie was always the instigator," remembered Ann Park, one of her close childhood friends; she would do and "dare anything; we would all follow along." Her cousin Lucy Challis, who lived next door, recalled that Amelia was always the most fun to play with; she "admired her ability, stood in awe of her information and intelligence," and "adored her imagination."

Amelia and her sister left that world behind in 1909 when they moved to Des Moines, Iowa. Their father had taken a job there in the claims department of the Chicago, Rock Island and Pacific railroad. It was a promising step for Edwin, who for years had been struggling to achieve some financial security. For a while, he had tinkered with an invention, hoping it might earn him a fortune, but another man, he discovered—after he'd squandered the family's tax money on the patent process—had invented the same mechanism two years earlier. In his new job, he and Amy hoped, the family would be able to climb out of debt and achieve some stability together.

For Amelia and Muriel, the move to Des Moines was an adventure. It was the first of many they would make as daughters of a "railroad man"—a life, Amelia wrote later, that taught her "the fascination of new people and new places" and of trying new things. Even in Des Moines, the Earharts moved often, setting up household in four homes in as many years. Their last house—near

ST. PAUL AND KANSAS CITY SHORT LINE RAILROAD COMPANY

1912   N° 722

Pass Mrs. E. S. Earhart and Two* dependent Daughters*****

ACCOUNT • Dependent. Family E.S.Earhart Claim Agent

ORDERED AND IONS ON BACK.

ERAL MANAGER

ST. PAUL & DES MOINES RAILROAD

1911

PASS —Mrs. E. S. Earhart & Family— Complimentary Rock Island Lines.

UNTIL DECEMBER 31ST 1911

N° 1062   Fredamemillon

VICE PRESIDENT & GENERAL MANAGER

Drake University in the prosperous Cottage Grove neighborhood—marked the peak of the family's material fortune. Amy was able to hire a maid and a cook, and Edwin, now head of the claims department and a specialist in railroad law, traveled to legal conferences across the Rock Island system in a luxurious private railroad car, staffed by a Japanese butler and cook. He frequently took his family along, convinced that travel was more beneficial for his daughters than formal schooling.

The family, in those days, often dressed in their best to hear concerts by some of the era's greatest musical stars, sponsored by Drake University. Clad in high-necked dresses, the girls would accompany their mother, in her rustling silk violet gown, and their father, in his stiff collar and Prince Albert coat, to the evening recitals. Afterward, Edwin and Amelia, who shared an "uncanny" ear for music, would sit together at the piano for an hour or more, playing by memory some of the pieces they had heard. Although Amelia was an able musician, she

hated to perform for others—"if she was playing or singing and anyone came in the room," Amy recalled, "she got up at once and stopped"—but she loved all kinds of music, from the German composers and grand opera to popular tunes.

The high points of family life were summer vacations. Edwin had discovered the town of Worthington, Minnesota—on the shores of Lake Okabena—on one of his journeys north, and for four summers the Earharts enjoyed "perfect" holidays there, boarding at the home of a Swedish family. Amelia and Muriel learned to ride horses fearlessly, saddled and bareback, and milked cows, played tennis, swam, and helped with the haying. Edwin took them fishing for lake bass, sunfish, and pickerel, and they had their first ride in an automobile, an REO motorcar that went "awfully fast," Amelia reported, at about ten miles an hour.

Left Between 1909 and 1913, a prosperous time, the Earharts settled into this home in Des Moines, Iowa.

Above Edwin and Amy Earhart

Edwin Earhart,
between 1915
and 1924

was strangely wrong. Edwin was walking slowly, setting each foot down carefully to keep his balance, and he had a "sickly smile" on his face as he lurched up the steps. The next day at church, Edwin seemed like himself and apologized to his family for his behavior the previous day. Despite many reassurances, however, he was soon stumbling home two or three times a week.

The effect on his family was crushing; their lighthearted, loving home life crumbled practically overnight. Amelia and Muriel grew skilled at avoiding their dad's "sickness." They learned to joke with Edwin only in the mornings, because he often came home from work raging about household expenses, Amy's family, the railroad, and virtually anything that caught his attention. Amelia and Muriel were too young to understand Edwin's behavior; they only knew, Muriel wrote, that their father did not seem to care for them anymore.

Edwin's drinking was not just a family problem; it was also wrecking his prospects and legal career. Errors began riddling his reports, and his supervisor started questioning his judgment and warning him to keep away from the "drinking crowd." Edwin's response to that advice, written after a few drinks, was hostile and scathing. He was promptly forced to resign and dispatched to a clinic for a month-long "cure" to strengthen his body and stiffen his willpower. Edwin arrived home from the hospital at the end of the month "bright-eyed and buoyant," grabbing Amy and waltzing her around the front hall while Amelia and Muriel laughed and clapped—happy and grateful to have their "old dad" back again.

After a few days, however, Edwin went back to the bottle, and things turned from bad to worse. In February 1912, Amy's mother, who had been suffering from a heart condition, passed away. Her death was a blow to Amelia, who was "choked

Already, however, forces were gathering that would shatter the security of Amelia's world and splinter her family. Edwin had started drinking on the road and, increasingly, in the office and after work. His dissolution became obvious one Saturday afternoon in 1911. Amelia, her sister, and ten of their friends were waiting in front of the Earhart house for Edwin to get off early from work and join them, as usual, in their neighborhood games. As he climbed off the streetcar, they raced to greet him, but they quickly sensed something

with grief inside," Amy remembered, though she "wasn't the kind of child to talk about it." With her grandmother's death—quickly followed by her grandfather's three months later—Amelia lost many of the physical ties to her happiest years. The old house on Quality Hill would be sold at auction, the barn would be torn down, and the garden would be subdivided for housing.

The deaths of Amelia and Alfred Otis had a dire impact, too, on Edwin and Amy. The Otises had left an estate valued at around $200,000, to be equally divided among their four living children. Because they had known about Edwin's drinking and unreliability, however, they instructed that Amy's share was to be held in trust for her for fifteen years, fearing that Edwin would squander the money. The news enraged him, inflaming his bitterness toward Amy's family, and he began brooding and drinking even more heavily to punish his wife. With his spreading reputation for boozing and erratic behavior, Edwin failed to convince Rock Island to reinstate him, and he had no luck landing claims jobs with other railroads. Finally, in the summer of 1913, he was offered a low-grade filing position in the freight office of the Great Northern Railway in St. Paul, Minnesota. Amy and the girls again packed their belongings and despondently left their lives in Des Moines for the new post. As their train to St. Paul was pulling out, Edwin sat drunken and slumped in a corner seat, and Muriel glimpsed tears of humiliation in her mother's eyes.

In St. Paul, the Earharts faced lean days of privation and poverty. The family rented a large house that had been vacant for years and watched every cent. Amy had to stretch her small income to cover all household expenses except rent, which Edwin paid from

his salary as a filing clerk. There was little left over to pay for the "staggering" coal bill they ran up during the long, harsh Minnesota winter, when the family huddled for warmth in two rooms of the

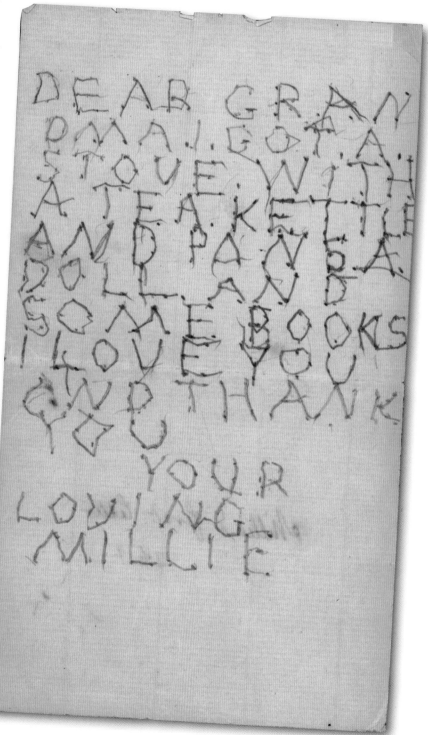

Amelia wrote this thank-you note to her grandmother when she was three or four.

THE GIRL IN BROWN WHO WALKS ALONE 15

frigid house. Meanwhile, Edwin was angling for a promotion. He announced to his family one day that he was "going back on the road" for the Great Northern to assess a wrecked train on the line, and he asked his daughters to pack his suitcase, as they used to do. Afterward, during supper, Amelia was unusually quiet. When she and her sister were clearing up, she showed Muriel an unopened bottle of whiskey she found when she was gathering together their father's things. The girls opened the seal and pulled out the cork, and Amelia started dumping the whiskey down the sink. Suddenly, Edwin appeared. Lunging for the empty bottle, he was about to strike Amelia when Amy came racing into the kitchen and grabbed his arm. Edwin, recovering himself, said that he had only wanted the liquor to "warm" himself a little on his journey. He left on the business trip, but received no offers of a promotion or better job.

It was a hard, isolating time. The Earharts had established friendships and roots in Des Moines, but in St. Paul they had few social connections. Acquaintances from church ignored them after token visits, and Amy's uncle—a wealthy, prominent member of St. Paul society—paid them one "duty call," then snubbed the Earharts as poor relations. Faced with no invitations to holiday parties at private homes, Amelia and Muriel were looking forward to a Twelfth Night gala held at their church—especially because Edwin, an exceptional waltzer, had promised to escort them and dance with each of them during the party. On the night of the gala, Amelia and Muriel waited for Edwin to return home from work before six o'clock, as he'd said he would. By eight o'clock, the girls were frantic, and about nine, when Edwin finally arrived home, Muriel burst into tears and ran up to her room. Amelia, however, showed no sign of distress or emotion. Instead, she strode calmly into the living room, took down the Christmas decorations, tore up the hand-painted holiday napkins, turned out the lights, and went upstairs to read in her room. There was no confrontation. Her father had disappointed her once again; it was no surprise.

Money problems worsened in the spring after Edwin, drunk, was struck by a car as he made his way, stumbling, across the street. Although he wasn't seriously injured, the $10 hospital bill was almost more than the family could afford, and there was no money left to buy spring clothes for the Earhart girls. Amelia, however, managed to "make do with cheerfulness." After rummaging in the attic, she came down carrying Amy's silk curtains from Des Moines. "Neither Amelia nor I liked to sew," Muriel wrote, and "we knew nothing about cutting material from a pattern," but Amelia had a keen eye and singular sense of style. She sent Pidge to buy dye, matching ribbons, and thread, then drew her design and cut out a pattern from newspapers. The homemade outfits were simple, and Amelia's sewing was hardly skilled, but they managed to pass muster in public—though the sisters tried to stay out of the rain so they wouldn't leave trails of dye on the sidewalk.

They were starting to make friends at church—where Amelia enjoyed singing in the choir—and at Central High School, where she enrolled as a junior. Amelia had always loved school and easily excelled, especially at mathematics. In grade school in Atchison, her headmistress observed, Amelia deduced the "correct answer to complex arithmetic problems but hates to put down the steps by which she arrives at the results." In high school, Amelia could easily do algebra in her head, but she preferred geometry because she had to work at it. She also loved Latin, physics, and chemistry, and she was setting her sights firmly on college. "I am going to B.M. [Bryn Mawr in

Pennsylvania]," she declared in a letter to her old friend Ginger Park, "if I have to drive a grocery wagon to accumulate the cash."

The year in St. Paul, however, ended on a depressing note. Late in the spring, Edwin thought he had been offered a legal job in the Burlington Railroad's Springfield, Missouri, office. The phone had finally begun to ring for Amelia and Muriel, but they "again packed all our belongings," Muriel wrote, "broke off friendships, and pulled up the roots we had just begun to put down in the last year." The move to Springfield, however, was a disaster. There was no job, Edwin discovered when they arrived— though the company charitably offered him a month's work while his family, now homeless and with little means of support, made other plans.

By now, three years of hardship and humiliation had nearly broken Amy. She had been a little hard of hearing since age sixteen when she had contracted typhoid fever. Now, however, she was noticeably deaf, her nerves were shot, and she had spells when she literally could not "get her legs to obey her." Back in St. Paul, Amelia had asked a doctor about her mother's condition; "anybody acting like that," he replied, "is on the verge of a nervous breakdown." Now, stranded in Springfield, Amy

Amelia at sixteen, in St. Paul, Minnesota

informed Edwin that she thought it best for the family to separate for a little while. She and the girls would stay with friends, the Shedd family in Chicago, until Edwin was able to establish a real home for them once again. Edwin objected at first, but the girls backed their mother, and he soon agreed. He would make his way back to Kansas City and open a law office, while Amy, Amelia, and Muriel moved to Illinois.

In Chicago, the Shedds welcomed Amy and the girls and gave them a home in the "graft-

When Amy separated from Edwin in 1914, she and the girls moved to Chicago, where Amelia enrolled in Hyde Park High School, shown here, under construction, in 1912.

ridden, beautiful, brash metropolis." Chicago seemed to them a "city for youth"; the demolition and construction Amelia and Muriel saw everywhere around them mirrored, in some ways, the uprooting and rebuilding they had been facing in their own lives. Eventually, Amy rented furnished rooms near the University of Chicago, and Muriel enrolled in Morgan Park High School, which she attended with Elizabeth Shedd. Amelia, however, refused to enroll in Morgan because its chemistry

lab, she complained, was a "kitchen sink." She was now focused on studying science and visited several Chicago high schools, inspecting their chemistry laboratories; in the end she selected Hyde Park High School, whose facilities seem to have met her demanding standards.

Amelia was a brilliant student, but she remained an outsider at the school, rarely interacting with her classmates. In Des Moines and St. Paul, she had been actively involved in the life of the school, playing basketball, attending plays and football games, and making friends. In Chicago, by contrast, Amelia kept to herself, heading straight home after school to look after her mother. When she did make her presence felt, it only further diminished her social standing. In her English class, her teacher, Mrs. Dingee, ignored the students while they clowned around and wasted the entire period. Amelia, outraged at the lack of seriousness, drafted a petition demanding that the school replace the elderly teacher—but when she asked her classmates to sign it, they grabbed the paper and tore it into pieces. Mrs. Dingee stayed in the classroom, and Amelia got a reputation as a "screwball."

Still, she refused to waste her time. By the third week of school, Amelia had convinced the librarian to let her read independently in the library and skip English class, and she earned credits by reading about four times as many books as the course required. Amelia graduated from Hyde Park High School in June, but she didn't go to commencement, and she was the only member of her class who refused to attend the senior banquet. Given her solitary, stiff-backed independence, it's no surprise that her peers captioned her yearbook photo "the girl in brown who walks alone."

Amelia had had to start over, again and again, in new cities and schools, her family had disintegrated, and her father, whom she had worshipped, had betrayed her love and confidence too many times. In Chicago, her natural resilience and enthusiasm essentially ran out. Head down, Amelia merely went through the motions that year and never even bothered to collect her diploma.

By now Amy felt it was time to reunite the family and rejoin Edwin, who had opened his own law practice in Kansas City. Amelia and Muriel were reluctant to go, but they dutifully boarded a train with their mother for Missouri. Edwin, who had been living with his seventy-two-year-old sister, was relieved to see them, and they moved into a modest house together on Charlotte Avenue. Edwin had finally stabilized his life, and he and Amy were working together to strengthen their financial prospects. It was critical, they realized, for Amy to take control of her inheritance. Her brother, Mark Otis, had been managing her trust—ineptly, as Amy's shrinking income indicated all too clearly; her $60,000 trust had dwindled to $45,000 in less than four years. Anxious to preserve funds for the girls' education, Amy filed suit in September 1915 to dissolve the trust that her parents had created.

Slowly, legal decisions began moving in her favor, and when Mark died a year and a half later, all the assets were finally turned over to Amy's control.

As her financial picture brightened, Amy made plans to continue her daughters' schooling. Although Amelia had long dreamed of enrolling in Bryn Mawr College, she now opted to postpone those plans and attend Ogontz, a prestigious girls' boarding school near Philadelphia. Heavily endowed, it drew well-off students, boasted its own art gallery, and hosted visits and lectures by famous artists and writers. For Amelia, the school offered the academic equivalent of a junior college experience that was stimulating

Amelia was fascinated with science and loved studying physics and chemistry.

Date _____ Name Amelia Earhart _____ Laboratory No. _____

Experiment No. I

Object To Test a Physical or Chemical Change

Apparatus Test-Tube; fumes.

Drawings and Sketches

Right In 1916, Amelia (left, with a couple of classmates) continued her studies at Ogontz, a prestigious boarding school for girls near Philadelphia.

Below A receipt for Amelia's books, excursions, and "entertainments" at Ogontz in 1917

CHECKS DRAWN TO THE OGONTZ SCHOOL

ABBY A. SUTHERLAND, Principal.

OGONTZ SCHOOL, PA., *June 11* 1917

Mr. *E. S. Earhart*

To **Ogontz School for Girls, Dr.**

NEAR PHILADELPHIA

TO CASH EXPENDED FOR *Miss Amelia Earhart* _____ DURING TERM

COMMENCING *February 1* 1917 CLOSING *May 29* 1917 AS FOLLOWS

Text Books

Wordsworth	
Byron	1 20
Burns	1 35
Hamlet	1 35
Othello	75
King Lear	75
Blue Prints; Photographs, Perry Pictures and Printed Slips for Art, etc.	75
Sheet Music	
Metronome Portfolio Harmony	2 15
Drawing Materials	
Medicine *Chaperonage*	1 28
Meals served in Nursery	
Chemicals for the Year	50
Chemistry Apron	
Excursions and Entertainments *Joan Slay* Physics Fee	25
Victor Talking Machine Co.	3 96
Treasure Island	2 53
Easter Recess Automobile	4 49
Joan the Woman 3.57 + 3.33	1 00
Gymnastic, Athletic and Military Equipment	6 90

and reviving. At last on her own, thousands of miles away from her family problems, she thrived at Ogontz and rediscovered her pleasure in socializing and school activities. Amelia's schedule, she reported a few weeks after she arrived in October 1916, was packed with studies and sports from seven in the morning until bedtime. "Every minute is accounted for," she told her mother; she had no time "for anything," she wrote with excitement, "because I want to get all possible."

"Did I tell you," she added, that "I have a reputation for brains?" Amelia had always been an intellectual, her mother remembered, and at Ogontz her unconventional intelligence was well rewarded. She placed into advanced French, earned good grades, and was inspired by the school's owner and headmistress, Abby Sutherland, a towering figure who had studied at Radcliffe with Helen Keller and Gertrude Stein. Amelia described Miss Sutherland as "a very brilliant woman, very impressive." She was taller than Amelia, who stood five foot eight, and "looked like a queen," a classmate remarked. Miss Sutherland recognized Amelia's wide-ranging scholarly interests, commenting that she was "always pushing into unknown seas in her reading" and that for the nineteen-year-old, literature "was an adventure." Although it seemed to Amelia that she hardly ever lifted her head out of a book, she made frequent trips to the theater, symphony, and opera and plunged into school sports, which she hadn't played since high school in St. Paul. In field hockey, she quickly became a high scorer and was invited to join Alpha Phi, an athletic sorority.

Ogontz was in the wooded, rolling hills of eastern Pennsylvania, and Amelia loved the "gorgeousness" of the school. One rainy day in spring, she was one of "only a few brave souls" who went out for a walk among the trees and wildflowers, and "it was splendid," she wrote, to be out in the wild weather, "to have the wind blow and the rain beat on your face." Amelia in general was "looking extremely well, and seems very happy," Miss Sutherland was able to report to Amy. "She has made a very warm place for herself in the hearts of her schoolmates and teachers by her charm of manner."

Amelia was beginning to look ahead at paths her life might possibly take, turning for inspiration to stories of women who were blazing new trails in professional life. She began assembling a scrapbook, cutting out newspaper and magazine articles about women lawmakers, veterinary surgeons, credit managers, trade union leaders, upholsterers, mental health workers, game wardens, and farmers in the U.S. and Europe, even women who were working as bank clerks and bookkeepers in Turkey. To Amelia, their particular occupation

didn't seem to matter. The women she chose had one point in common—they were pioneers.

Her horizons were also expanding in other ways. That summer, after visiting her parents in Kansas City, she traveled north to Camp Gray, a resort on Lake Michigan, where she vacationed with friends for a couple of weeks. There, perhaps for

the first time, she socialized somewhat freely with "lovely" young men—including Ken, who was "very nice and sensitive and almost brilliant," Gordon, who took "several dozen" photographs of her, and Harry, who wanted to take Amelia and her friend Sarah to Chicago. It was a "wildly exciting time" Amelia wrote, within the bounds of convention.

With its sophisticated focus on art and literature, Ogontz challenged Amelia and developed her leadership talents.

Above and opposite In the summer of 1917 Amelia had a "wildly exciting time" on Lake Michigan with "lovely" young men, including Kenneth Merrill.

In August, she reported, one boy who had left the lake was planning to come back to see her—but without her friend Sarah there, Amelia admitted, "I should not feel quite comfortable." Still, she wrote that the attention from "such nice boys" that summer made for "ideal times" canoeing, hiking, swimming, and walking on the beach.

Amelia returned to Ogontz in the fall "bursting" with health and happiness and increasingly confident of her own powers. She was busier than ever—"the more one does," she wrote, "the more one can do"—and made a number of principled, and not always popular, stands. She hated the fact that sororities excluded some girls and approved when Miss Sutherland abolished the secret societies. Firm in her beliefs, Amelia did not hesitate to criticize schoolmates who started agitating to

reinstate the organizations. Although she believed she had "lost all my friends or a good many for jumping on them so," her leadership qualities were obvious to many of her peers. They voted Amelia vice president of her class, and they selected her to compose a new school song. Amelia also penned the class motto, "Honor is the foundation of courage," and was one of five students elected to a board overseeing the school's honor system. Again, Amelia did battle, this time with Miss Sutherland, who wanted to include faculty members and some of her favorite students—"whom no one can abide," Amelia remarked—on the Honor Board. "I nearly had my head taken off," she said of her bruising clash with the headmistress. Amelia also rebelled against the school's intellectual limits. Ogontz students, she argued, should be able to read about and discuss any topic that interested them, no matter how unconventional or controversial.

The war, too, was now absorbing her time and energy. In April 1917 America had entered World War I, and that fall, Amelia helped organize a Red Cross chapter at Ogontz, knitted sweaters for the troops, and took a special training course in surgical dressings. Ogontz, however, remained a secluded respite from the personal conflicts and upheaval she had experienced for many years. Her frequent uprootings had made her adept at dealing with new people and situations, but they had also reinforced her natural self-sufficiency and tendency to hold herself apart and "walk alone." Amelia, as she put it, was a rolling stone—and rolling, she reflected, "left its mark on me."

2
VAGABONDING

FRANCE ITALY MALTA GIBRA... SALON...

EGYPT ...ESOPOTAMIA HOLLAND ...VITZERLAND RUSSIA

V.A.D.
NURSING MEMBERS, COOKS, KITCHEN-MAIDS, CLERKS, HOUSE-MAIDS, WARD-MAIDS, LAUNDRESSES, MOTOR-DRIVERS, ETC.
ARE URGENTLY NEEDED
APPLICATION TO BE MADE TO

The shock of war soon disrupted the sheltered safety of Amelia's life. During Christmas break in 1917, she visited Toronto, where Muriel was studying at St. Margaret's School to prepare for enrollment at Smith College. Although America had only recently entered World War I, Canadian troops had been fighting on the front lines for three brutal years, and Toronto's hospitals were teeming with casualties. The city's parks and sidewalks, too, were crowded with the walking wounded. Strolling with her sister one day, Amelia was stunned to see four one-legged men struggling down the street together on crutches. War, she saw instantly, wasn't about knitting sweaters, rolling bandages, or selling Liberty bonds; it was about young men killed or horribly injured, blinded and crippled in the prime of life. Returning to school, she abruptly decided, would be "impossible"; war was everywhere she looked, and she had to help.

Weeks later, Amelia dropped out of Ogontz. She and Muriel took an apartment together, and Amelia threw herself into first aid training classes with the Canadian Red Cross—going to lectures and taking V.A.D. (Voluntary Aid Detachment) and home nursing courses, intent, she said, on "getting everything I can." She even planned to see an operation, she announced, "if I can wheadle anybody into letting me."

By April, she was putting her skills to work as a nurse's aide at Spadina Military Hospital. "Sister Amelia" was popular with her patients, who were recovering from shell shock, shrapnel injuries, poison gas burns, and other miseries of trench warfare on the Western Front. Her duties involved everything from scrubbing floors and carrying trays to playing tennis with convalescing patients, and there were always, she added, some "lovely" backs to be rubbed. With her knowledge of chemistry, she was soon promoted to the dispensary, where her lab skills and distaste for medicinal whiskey made her exceptionally useful.

Opposite Amelia, in flying helmet and pearls, in 1925

Above In early 1918, during World War I, Amelia dropped out of Ogontz and moved to Toronto, Canada, to take Voluntary Aid Detachment (V.A.D.) training classes and work as a nurse's aid in a hospital for wounded soldiers.

Amelia's tasks as a uniformed "merry sunshine" lasted from seven in the morning till seven at night, and the drudgery often made the days drag. Life in the provincial capital, however, wasn't all dull. Amelia had friends and suitors, went to concerts and hockey games, and loved to go riding with Muriel whenever she could, splurging on rented horses at a local stable. Amelia became fond of a "devil" of a stallion named Dynamite, a powerful steed famous for bucking his riders.

Amelia (right) and a friend at Spadina Military Hospital in Toronto

Every afternoon for weeks, she would stop by the stables for a while, gentling the irascible horse with apples and kindness. Soon, she was riding him masterfully and impressing other riders with her bravery.

One of them, an officer in the Royal Flying Corps, so admired her horsemanship that he invited her to watch him fly his plane out at Armor Heights, a military airfield on the edge of town.

There, for the first time, Amelia saw planes soaring and circling, graceful as gulls, and something quickened inside her. She had seen a plane once before—at the Iowa State Fair, when she was eleven—but the contraption of rusty wire and wood hadn't impressed her. Now, at twenty, she was suddenly swept off her feet by the romance and excitement of aviation. The risks involved, too, were unexpectedly thrilling. Soon after, at a stunt-flying show, a pilot wanted to scare her by diving his small plane right at her, trying to make her run. Amelia stayed where she was in the path of the plane, filled with a strangely intoxicating mixture of fear and pleasure. She knew it was inevitable that she would fly, but she would have to be patient. The Royal Flying Corps banned civilian passengers, so Amelia did the next best thing—she spent nearly every free hour at the airfield, absorbing it all.

Illness, however, soon sidelined her passion for aviation. A deadly flu epidemic, brought home to Toronto by returning troops, spread quickly and catastrophically through the city. Hospitals were packed with patients, and doctors and nurses, many stricken themselves, were stretched to the breaking point. Despite the contagion, Amelia volunteered to work long days and nights, ladling out medicine from buckets in an overflowing pneumonia ward. By early November, Amelia, too, was hospitalized with influenza, pneumonia, and a pneumococcal infection inside her cheekbone. Since antibiotics weren't yet available, the only treatment was to surgically open and "wash out" the affected sinus. It was a painful, debilitating procedure, and it took her months to recover.

In February 1919, when she was healthy enough to travel, Amelia left Toronto and moved to Northampton, Massachusetts, where Muriel was continuing college preparatory studies. Still weak and recovering, Amelia at first chafed at her

"Whileaway"

Looking from golf links.

"enforced idleness," but she was soon well enough to take a course for women, sponsored by Smith College, in automobile repair, gaining her first hands-on experience with engines.

In the spring, Amy, too, made the move to Northampton. Edwin had overcome his alchoholism and now wanted to move from Kansas City to Los Angeles, where his law practice, he believed, would have better prospects. Amy, who had struggled through so much upheaval, was not eager or ready to move again and wanted to spend time with her daughters before joining Edwin. Since she had come into some family money, she and the girls decided to rent a cottage for the entire summer at fashionable Lake George, a mountain resort in upstate New York. There, during the long, lazy months, Amelia became friendly with the Stablers, a family that was vacationing in a nearby cottage. When twenty-three-year-old Marian Stabler first met Amelia up at the lake, she was impressed by the "tall, very slim girl in a blue suit" with "slow Western speech" and a "serious expression." Amelia was still pale from her illness, with circles under her eyes; she wore no

With her mother and sister, Amelia (top) spent the summer of 1919 vacationing in the resort community of Lake George in upstate New York.

makeup, Marian recalled, and had "an unusual combination of boyish straight-forwardness" and "strangely poetic beauty."

Amelia, Muriel, Marian, and her brother, Frank—a navy veteran and senior at Williams College—spent the warm days together playing tennis, swimming, canoeing, dancing to gramophone records, and listening to avant-garde poetry composed by another of their young neighbors, Mark Turbyfill. Amelia, Marian observed, was a "very poetic" person with "serious aesthetic ideas." She was also starting to make ambitious plans for her own future. Amelia's nursing experience in Toronto had given her "a yen for medicine," and she was now thinking she might want to become a doctor.

In the fall of 1919, while Muriel entered Smith College as a freshman, Amelia left for New York City and enrolled as a premed student in Columbia University's extension program. She registered for a full schedule of lectures and lab courses—all of the "ologies"—at both Columbia and Barnard College, plus an extra "luxury course" she added in French literature. It was a heavy academic load, but she made good grades and earned the respect of her peers and teachers. According to her biology professor, Amelia was a "stimulating student"; she "grasped the significance of an experiment, mentally assayed the results, and drew conclusions while I was still lecturing about setting up the experimental machinery." Amelia even volunteered to serve as a medical guinea pig, letting her bacteriology professor inoculate her with experimental serums in an effort to cure what had now become a chronic infection inside her cheekbone. According to Marian Stabler, who was also in New York studying art, she "took millions of bugs in the arm, on the principle that it couldn't make her any worse"

and her teacher might learn something scientifically useful in the process.

Amelia was studying hard, with little money to spend, but she was also, as usual, having a good time. She rented a furnished room on Morningside Drive, went horseback riding in Central Park, and spent much of her free time exploring the city and "every nook and cranny" of the university, including its hidden maze of underground tunnels. Amelia also set her sights on much higher ground. Ignoring gawkers, she and her closest friend at Columbia, Louise de Schweinitz, climbed into the lap of a huge seated statue of a woman on the library steps, where they sat reading poetry and blithely eating cherries out of a paper bag. Amelia also managed to get her hands

As a premed student at Columbia University in 1919 and 1920, Amelia loved exploring the school's underground tunnels and climbing the steep library dome.

on the secret key to the library's domed roof. More than once, Louise recalled, she followed behind Amelia up endless steps and over the steep dome, on their hands and knees, to the very top, while students below stared and applauded. Up there on their dizzying perch, 105 feet above Amsterdam Avenue, Broadway, and the Cathedral of St. John the Divine, the two of them sat and talked about serious matters. Amelia, Louise remembered, never confided anything about her love life, but she did share strong feelings about marriage. "I can think of lots of things worse than never getting married," Amelia told her, "and one of the worst is being married to a man who tied you down. I'm not sold on marriage at all for myself, but, of course," she added, "I'm not in love with anybody—yet."

Amelia, in the eyes of her friend, had "tremendous ability and determination" and could have done anything in life she wanted to. Abruptly, however, in May 1920, Amelia dropped out of Columbia and abandoned her plans to become a doctor. She explained, unconvincingly, that she lacked some of the practical, bedside skills that physicians need. The more likely reason for her decision, however, was family pressure. Edwin had been lobbying hard for his wife and daughters to move to Los Angeles. He had joined the Christian Science Church, whose members had helped him beat alcohol addiction, and he was establishing a reputation for himself and his legal practice. Edwin was feeling so positive about his future that he was thinking about running for the state legislature, and he wanted to have his family there by his side.

Amelia reluctantly agreed to join Edwin, and she convinced Amy, who was still in New England,

to move west with her to California. Muriel, however, was intent on staying at Smith College, so Amelia, at twenty-three, took on the task of trying to patch up her parents' unhappy marriage. After that, she told Muriel, she was determined to return to the East Coast and live her own life again.

Los Angeles, however, proved to have compelling attractions. The family's two-story house

Columbia classmate Louise de Schweinitz (right) often accompanied Amelia on her adventures around New York City.

on West Fourth Street was spacious and pleasant, and the climate, for Amelia, was close to ideal. She loved tennis, horseback riding, and just about anything she could do in the open air, and L.A. was a mecca for all kinds of outdoor activities. With its clear skies and wide-open terrain, it was also a fast-growing center for aviation. Nearly everyone around, it seemed, was fascinated with flying, including many of Hollywood's biggest stars and studio heads. Amelia started taking her father with her to every flying exhibition in the area, craning her neck in the crowds to watch daredevils spinning, swooping, and diving in old military planes.

At the first air meet she and Edwin attended, at Daugherty Field, the sky was blue, flying conditions were perfect, and Amelia had made up her mind—she wanted to fly. Edwin, wilting in the

Above Amelia abandoned her pre-medical studies in 1920 and moved to Los Angeles, where her parents rented this comfortable house and tried to patch up their failing marriage.

Right Muriel (left) enjoys a day at the beach in Santa Monica with Amelia.

heat and dust, wasn't nearly as keen on aviation as his daughter, but he gamely arranged for Amelia to take a ten-minute trial hop at another field. When they arrived at Rogers Airport the next day for her appointment, a former army pilot named Frank Hawks settled Amelia in the front cockpit of the airplane for her first flight—along with a second pilot, just in case she turned out to be a "nervous lady" and wanted to jump out of the plane. Amelia, however, wasn't a fearful flyer; she was completely sold. By the time they were a few hundred feet off the ground, soaring high over the ocean and the Hollywood Hills, she knew that she had to learn how to fly on her own. Even as a child, she recalled,

she'd known that life was too short for all the fun and excitement there was to enjoy. Learning how to fly was something Amelia couldn't put off; by the time she landed, she was ready to sign up for instruction at any price.

That evening, she casually mentioned to her parents that she wanted to take flying lessons, "knowing full well," she remembered, that "I'd die if I didn't." Edwin at first was supportive. "When do you start?" he offhandedly asked, but he balked when he found out the cost—$500 for ten to twelve hours of instruction. Amy, though, was more sympathetic, especially after Amelia offered to earn her own money to pay for the expensive lessons.

In the early 1920s, stunt-flying shows—featuring aerial acrobatics, wing-walking, and other daredevil maneuvers—were all the rage.

Amelia's next step was finding the right kind of teacher. She wanted to work with a woman, thinking she'd be less self-conscious, and she'd heard of a female pilot, Neta Snook, who gave lessons at an airfield south of L.A.

Neta never forgot the day Edwin and Amelia first came out to Kinner Field, a 210-acre stretch of dirt and weeds surrounded by vegetable farms. Amelia looked improbably elegant in a brown suit and silk scarf, carrying white gloves in her long-fingered hands and wearing braids wrapped around her head in a golden coil. The tall, slim young woman looked like a finishing-school girl, but Neta—clad in grimy overalls and covered with grease—liked her on sight. "I want to fly," Amelia told her straightforwardly. "Will you teach me?" Neta, just a year older than Amelia, was happy to help. At twenty-four, "Snooky," as everyone called her, was already an enterprising, independent full-time pilot. Originally a midwestwerner like Amelia, she was the first woman ever accredited by Virginia's Curtiss School of Aviation and had bought and rebuilt her own biplane, a wrecked military Canuck, after the war. Now, she was making a good living in Los Angeles giving lessons, doing aerial advertisements, test-flying planes, and taking paying customers up for rides and flying tours of local towns and attractions.

The very next day, on January 3, 1921, Neta gave her serious new student a first lesson. Amelia arrived at the field this time wearing brown riding jodhpurs, lace-up boots, and a tight-fitting jacket—"a beautifully tailored outfit," Neta recalled—with a library book on aerodynamics under her arm. After some initial instruction, she had climbed into the cockpit and learned how to taxi a plane. Within a month, she was thoroughly hooked on flying; Amelia had logged four hours of flight time, and Kinner Field was a second home. There wasn't much there—just a hangar and wind sock on a big, barren lot—but it also had airplanes and the carefree camaraderie of pilots, plane lovers,

Amelia (right) and her first flying instructor, Neta Snook, pose in front of the Kinner Airster, a sport plane Amelia purchased in 1921.

Chemical engineer Sam Chapman (far right) boarded at the Earharts' home and dated Amelia.

and would-be flyers. On days when it was too foggy or windy to go up, friends would come by with armloads of corn or potatoes from surrounding farms, and they'd cook up a makeshift feast on the field's wood-burning stove, chatting about planes and adventure and "ground flying" for hours.

Amelia admired Neta, who, she said, was a "top-notch" flyer, dressed and talked like a man, and could do everything around a plane that a man could do. The two young women quickly became close companions. Neta sometimes shared meals and stayed over at the Earharts' home, where Amy and Edwin made her feel like another daughter. "Mother Earhart," Neta remembered, was "warm and friendly," although she was hard of hearing. After dinner, the family would usually read or play cards, and Neta and Edwin would have serious talks that frequently touched on Amelia. Edwin worried about his daughter's flying, but he was very proud of "Meelie," who "has a wonderful brain," he remarked to Neta. "She'll go far."

Later, in the privacy of Amelia's room, the two friends would often talk about love and marriage. Neta had a serious boyfriend, and she remembered that Amelia once gave her a piece of hardheaded advice. "Are you sure you're ready to give up your career?" Amelia asked, because if they married, she warned, her man was the type who would always "insist on being boss."

Amelia, too, had romantic interests. One of them was a chemical engineer named Samuel Chapman, a quiet intellectual with dark hair and quick blue eyes who was boarding at the Earhart home with two other young men. She and Sam, a Tufts graduate from Marblehead, Massachusetts, were attracted to each other and had much in common, including tennis, swimming, and a love of literature. Amelia dated others, too, usually when she and Snooky set out to explore out-of-the-way ethnic neighborhoods in Los Angeles, which they loved to do. Neta, especially, felt more comfortable if they brought dates along, but Amelia always had "strict scruples" about the arrangements. "She didn't feel it was right for a boy to spend time and money on her," Neta recalled, "if she, in turn, felt no interest in him"; Amelia looked at it as a form of stealing. She also, Neta observed, preferred

on men than on airplanes. Ever since her first trip to Kinner Field, she had been watching its owner, Bert Kinner, tinkering with a fast little sport plane he was building, which he called the Airster. Amelia had logged "the tremendous total of two and one-half hours' instruction," she later

Top Restored 1920s biplane

Right The Kinner Airster was a fast, innovative plane that took off "like a sandpiper."

older men. Once, when they took a day trip to the mountains with two boys and got stuck in a violent rainstorm as it was getting dark, Amelia refused to find a place to spend the night and demanded that they drive two hundred miles in the raging downpour back to Los Angeles. "Mature men," she insisted to Neta, "would never have put us through such an ordeal."

In general, however, Amelia had little patience for "frivolous doings" if it was a good day for flying, and she was usually less focused

recalled, when she decided that her life would be incomplete unless she possessed the plane. Unlike

Neta's Canuck, which was heavy, slow, and under-powered, Kinner's new plane was fast and light and hopped off quickly "like a sandpiper" when it took off. It was less than half the weight of the Canuck, due to its innovative air-cooled engine, and so maneuverable that Amelia could lift its tail and move it anywhere she wanted to around the field.

The Airster was "the prettiest plane we had ever seen," Neta remarked, but she and other pilots warned Amelia not to buy it, worried that it lacked stability and power. Amelia, however, was smitten with the plane and wouldn't change her mind. The Airster was a costly infatuation at $2,000—a huge sum at a time when a Model T Ford cost around $370 and a Canuck could be had for less than $1,000. Although Edwin at first promised to help pay for the plane, he changed his mind after Amelia had already signed the sales contract and given Bert Kinner a down payment. So Amelia used up all of her savings, and Muriel's, too, to purchase the plane and got a job in a telephone company mailroom to help pay off the balance. Her salary was hardly enough to make a dent, but her initiative impressed Amy, who also contributed a few hundred dollars—provided that Amelia resign from the mailroom and "stay home a little." Amelia did, but she soon took another paying job as a telephone operator since, as she was

rapidly learning, the reality of aviation was "no job, no pay, no fly. Job, pay, fly."

In July 1921, just before her twenty-fourth birthday, Amelia owned the bright yellow biplane,

which she named "The Canary." It was, she remembered, her "first love," and she and her family treated it "like a favorite pony," Amy recalled. "We said goodnight to it and patted its nose and almost fed it apples." From then on, Amelia remembered, "the family scarcely saw me for I worked all the

Amelia used all her savings and took a job as a telephone operator to help pay for the Airster, which she painted bright yellow and called "The Canary."

By 1922, Amelia was making head-lines as a "society girl-student aviatrix."

week and spent what I had of Saturday and Sunday at the airport a few miles from town."

The plane was an expensive responsibility, given the heavy costs of storage, maintenance, and gasoline. Fortunately, Bert Kinner offered her free hangar space and mechanical help, since Amelia was happy to demonstrate the Airster for potential customers. And although she had to learn to fly "all over again" in the little biplane, which was "like a leaf in the air" and "not for a beginner," Snooky generously continued Amelia's flying lessons for free.

Safety was also a growing concern now that she owned her own plane, and Amelia rarely took passengers up with her in the Airster. "If I crashed," she explained, "it was my own responsibility and it was my own property that was being injured"; she wanted to be absolutely sure of herself, she said, before "I whisk anybody else's body around." Crashes, as she knew, happened all too often in the fragile, flimsy,

unstable aircraft of the time. Aces and daredevils, as well as novices, often had hair-raising near-misses and close brushes with death, and Amelia, when she was flying her Airster with Neta, had two frightening crack-ups of her own. The first time, her plane climbed too slowly after takeoff, due to a malfunction, and would have slammed into a grove of trees if Amelia hadn't deliberately gone into a stall. Thinking quickly, she shut off the engine before hitting the ground, avoiding a fire, and she and Neta walked away without injuries. Another time, they both carelessly neglected to check the plane's fuel level before taking off, and the Airster, out of gas, crashed in a cabbage patch. The impact damaged the propeller and landing gear, and Amelia bit her tongue badly when they hit the ground.

Partly due to these experiences, perhaps, Amelia was in no hurry to pilot her plane solo. Snooky felt she was ready, after she had logged almost five hours in the Canuck and four hours in the Airster, but Amelia, for some reason, kept putting it off. She may have been remembering something her father had taught her when she was a child—that knowledge is often the best cure for fear. Amelia, applying this rule, wanted to learn as much as she could about the perils of flying before she went up on her own. She felt she needed more training—to learn everything she could about getting her plane into, and out of, all kinds of dangerous situations. That meant learning stunt flying, with all its spins, stalls, dives, and other risky maneuvers. Unless she had actually experienced and recovered from these situations, she would never really know in her bones how to do it, and she wanted to become so familiar with them that she'd never even have to think. For Amelia, Neta's teaching, it seemed, was merely phase one. The next step was advanced training, and she started taking stunting lessons from a former World War I flying ace named John Montijo.

By then Muriel had come to Los Angeles for her summer vacation, and she would often go out to the airfield with Amelia to watch her train and learn more about her sister's engrossing new occupation. It was a lengthy journey—over an hour to the end of the streetcar line, then a hike of several miles down a long, dusty highway. On Sundays, they'd bring along a basket of sandwiches and a chocolate cake that Amy had baked for the airfield regulars—"Bohemians," Muriel called them, who were devoted to flying and considered a bit crazy by the general public. In the blazing one-hundred-degree heat and heady fumes of gas and engine grease, Muriel would pitch in by shellacking the canvas wings or replacing the rusty guide wires on Neta's plane, while pilots took joyriders up or traded stories in the cool shade of a shed.

After weeks of stunt flying lessons, Amelia at last decided she was ready to solo. It was by no means an ideal performance. On her first attempt, a shock absorber broke as she was taking off, and she had to stop abruptly and repair her plane. The second time, she took off and climbed five thousand feet before executing a landing that was, she admitted, "thoroughly rotten." Although the flight was nothing to be proud of, Amelia was now really a pilot, free to fly on her own, in her own plane, whenever she could.

She was also beginning to look, more and more, like a genuine aviator, one of those high-flying heroes who were capturing the public's imagination. Always careful and conscious about her appearance, Amelia bought the classic accoutrements—a helmet, a pair of goggles, and a patent leather coat that she deliberately aged by rubbing off the shine, streaking it with oil stains, and sleeping in it for three nights to give it proper

wrinkles. She also began cutting her hair—secretly, a few snips at a time, so her mother wouldn't notice—then curling her straight locks to make them look "naturally" tousled. Dressed in her trousers—which showed off her boyish slimness

Dressed in jodhpurs and tie, she was starting to develop her impeccable, androgynous trademark style.

and hid the "piano legs" she detested, with their shapeless ankles—Amelia must have known that she cut a dashing figure. The effect was nothing at all like the disheveled, mannish look Neta adopted. As one pilot put it, "we were not quite sure as to whether 'Snooky' was a man or woman, as few of us ever saw her except in a pair of dirty coveralls, her reddish hair closely cropped, and her freckled face usually made up with the

assistance of airport dust and a dash of grease." Amelia, however, always looked unmistakably feminine in her breeches and boots, and beautifully put together.

She was following her passion, and she was starting to attract public attention. Women pilots were rare in the masculine flying community, and they challenged common notions about the "gentler sex." Amelia undoubtedly knew that female flyers made headlines; after her first crash, Neta saw her powdering her nose, explaining that she had to "look nice" when reporters came. Now, it was Amelia's growing fame as an aviatrix that was making news. In December 1921, she was a star of the invitation-only Pacific Coast Ladies Derby, appearing along with silent-movie star Aloysia McLintic. Eight months later, in August 1922, the *Los Angeles Examiner* published a half-page picture of Amelia, posed with her Airster, with an article that lauded her as a pretty "society girl-student aviatrix." Amelia, in the interview, modestly said she didn't "crave publicity"; still, she added, it would be "the greatest fun" to fly across the country, perhaps dropping in at Vassar College to take a postgraduate course. In October, the *New York Times*, too, ran a glamorous photo of Amelia, a "Columbia Co-Ed," in her goggles and still somewhat shiny leather coat, describing her "Post-Graduate Activities" as piloting her own plane out in California.

With all the flattering publicity she was getting, Amelia may have felt driven to demonstrate her real skills as a pilot. That month, she invited Edwin and Muriel to an air show but told them she couldn't sit with them during the event. They didn't know why—until an announcer declared that a young lady was going to try to set an altitude record in her own biplane. Amelia hadn't mentioned the attempt, in case she didn't succeed. But the day was clear, the sky was blue, and she flew easily to around thirteen thousand feet. After that, however, her Airster ran into mechanical trouble. As she was climbing fifty feet a minute, her plane started knocking and vibrating violently, and she knew she had to come down. Amelia had been flying for almost an hour, and her father and sister were getting worried. When she landed, however, "there was great rejoicing," she recalled, because she had set an official women's altitude record of fourteen thousand feet. Amelia modestly claimed she "wouldn't have cared about the record" except that it might help Bert Kinner sell airplanes—but

her achievement made the newspaper, and she kept the clipping.

The new record didn't last long. Another pilot, Ruth Nichols, broke it several weeks later, and Amelia followed up with another attempt. This time, however, when she climbed above ten thousand feet, she flew into clouds, sleet, and dense, heavy fog. The conditions disoriented her, and she couldn't gauge her position in space. It was impossible to climb farther, so Amelia put her plane into a tailspin and dove down to three thousand feet, where she finally emerged from the fog bank and landed safely. A veteran pilot who watched her performance was not impressed—if there had been fog all the way down to the ground, he said, she might have killed herself.

Seven months later, Amelia polished her credentials as a serious flyer. On May 16, 1923, she passed the certification test to receive her pilot's license from the Fédération Aéronautique Internationale (FAI), the world governing body of aviation. Amelia was the sixteenth women in the world to earn a license issued by the FAI and the first woman to receive one from its U.S. affiliate, the National Aeronautic Association (NAA). The following month, she joined the ranks of elite flyers in the worldwide Aeronautical Hall of Fame.

She was enjoying freedom and growing celebrity in the sky, but life on the ground was a vexing reality check, mainly because money was a constant issue. Aviation was an expensive hobby, and to support it, Amelia held a string of jobs—working in her father's office and the telephone company and even doing a stint as a truck driver, hauling building materials. After taking a photography course at the University of Southern California, she also worked for three months in a commercial photography lab and managed to sell a photo she was lucky enough to snap of a gushing oil well.

Opposite left
Along with other female flyers, including silent-screen star Aloysia McLintic, Amelia (right) was performing at local air shows and winning public attention

Opposite right
Amelia stands next to McLintic's plane, wearing a patent-leather coat she deliberately aged by staining it and sleeping in it to give it proper wrinkles.

FÉDÉRATION AÉRONAUTIQUE
INTERNATIONALE

NATIONAL AERONAUTIC
ASSOCIATION OF U.S.A.
INC.

Certificate No. **6017**

The above named Association, recognized
by the Fédération Aéronautique Internationale, as the governing authority for the
United States of America, certifies that

Amelia M. Earhart

born *24th* day of *July,* *1898*
having fulfilled all the conditions required by
the Fédération Aéronautique Internationale,
for an Aviator Pilot is hereby brevetted
as such.

Dated *May 16,* *1923*
CONTEST COMMITTEE

F. R. Lahm
Chairman
B. Russell Shaw
Executive Vice-Chairman

Amelia M. Earhart

In 1923, she was the first woman to earn a pilot's license from the National Aeronautic Association (the document misstates her birth year as 1898 instead of 1897).

The Earharts' money problems, however, were much bigger than Amelia's flying habit. After paying Muriel's tuition for her junior year, they realized that Amy's inheritance had dwindled to $20,000. They needed to rebuild their principal and thought they had an exceptional opportunity, thanks to one of Sam Chapman's connections. His friend Peter Barnes, a civil engineer, was a partner in a gypsum mine near Moapa, Nevada. Peter had come to L.A. hoping to raise about $20,000 to buy two trucks and improve the road from his mine to the nearest railroad. Bankers weren't interested, but the Earharts, with Amelia's encouragement, thought the gypsum mine might be their "bonanza," and Amy invested all her remaining money in Peter's business. Months later, when Muriel was at Smith

College, she received a letter from Amelia, special delivery, with devastating news. "There is no way that I can soften the blow for you," Amelia said. There had been a flood up at the mine; Peter was drowned, one of the trucks was destroyed, and the mine itself was totally washed out. "All of Mother's investment is gone," Amelia wrote, and the family was "reeling from the blow."

Everywhere, it seemed, there was more bad news. Muriel was forced to drop out of college and return to L.A., where she found employment as a fourth-grade teacher. Amelia made the wrenching decision to sell her Canary and bought a new hauling truck with a partner as an investment; the reckless new owner of the plane, on his very first flight, took a friend up with him and crashed, killing them both. And in 1924 Amelia fell ill once again with her old sinus infection, which was raging and more painful than ever. She had to endure another operation at a cost of $500, which she couldn't afford. With all the family hardship and financial stress, the Earharts' marriage, too, was finally coming apart. In the spring, Edwin decided to file for divorce. Amy chose not to contest it, and she and her daughters moved out of the family home and into a small house they rented together on Sunset Boulevard.

For years, Amelia had dreamed of flying across the country to the East Coast—hopscotching across deserts, pastures, and dirt landing strips— and she had even assembled maps and data for the marathon flight. Muriel, too, was eager to return east and continue her studies, and Amy had never been particularly happy in California. It seemed like the right moment to make a move. Amelia, over time, had managed to buy a second airplane—a single-seat Kinner—but her health was now so delicate that she realized she would never be able to complete a cross-country flight. Instead,

she sold her plane and bought herself a car—not just any automobile, but a sleek, second-hand 1922 Kissel, a low-slung, bright yellow roadster with black fenders. Three years earlier, Neta had taught her to drive in a rented Model T Ford, and ever since, Amelia loved driving almost as much as she loved flying. Now, in June 1924—while Muriel went east by train in time to start summer classes at Harvard—Amelia loaded her mother and their belongings into the Kissel, and they set off on a cross-continental trek.

As they left L.A., Amy asked her which way they were going. "I'm going to surprise you," Amelia replied, heading the car north rather than east. Since neither of them had seen many national parks, Amelia wanted to do some circuitous touring, over rugged two-lane roads, as they crossed the country. They stopped at Sequoia, Yosemite, and Crater Lake, then turned north into Canada, seeing Banff and Lake Louise, then south again, down into Yellowstone. The spontaneous trip must have delighted Amy, an adventurous traveler who loved ending up "in strange places and at strange

In 1924, after selling her plane, she bought a 1922 Kissel roadster, a bright yellow touring car like this 1920 Kissel Gold Bug.

hours" when she was on the road. By the time they arrived in Boston many weeks later, they had driven a total of seven thousand miles, and the Kissel's windshield was plastered with tourist stickers.

Muriel, in the meantime, had found a job teaching junior high school in Medford, Massachusetts, and Amelia and Amy moved into a two-story house with her in the Boston suburb. Three days after arriving, however, Amelia—who must have been suffering badly on the last leg of the drive—entered Massachusetts General Hospital for another surgery. This time, doctors took out a small piece of bone, allowing her sinus to drain naturally and relieving the constant, agonizing pain she'd been experiencing.

In June 1924, after her parents divorced, Amelia and her mother left Los Angeles for Boston on a winding seven-thousand-mile car trip through Yellowstone and other national parks.

Although she was weak and debilitated from the operation, Amelia started looking ahead. Again, she needed to begin over, and this time she thought about studying engineering. In the fall, she returned to New York, intending to re-enroll in Columbia, but she was still frail and exhausted from her infection and so broke that she went without everything, Marian Stabler recalled, to pay for the upkeep on her beloved Kissel. She spent weeks convalescing with Marian at her home on Long Island, where the two friends talked "about everything under the sun," except Amelia's personal life and painful family issues. She never mentioned anything, Marian later recounted, about her parents' divorce, her father's drinking, or her lack of funds.

Finally, in January 1925, Amelia was feeling strong enough to climb the steep dome of Columbia's Low Library once again, and in February, she registered and paid the fees for two courses, physics and intermediate algebra. It was a much lighter academic load than she had carried in her first year as a student, and it was very likely all that she could pay for. Her funds were so depleted, it turned out, that she couldn't continue. Two months later, in April, she withdrew from Columbia for the last time. Broke and dispirited, Amelia drove back to Boston, where at least she would be able to live rent-free with Muriel and Amy. She had managed to earn a respectable B in physics, but she left with a disappointing C- in her algebra class. Since her poor showing in math might derail her plans for an engineering degree, Amelia opted to retake the course at Harvard's summer school. This time she earned an encouraging A and decided to apply for admission and a scholarship to the Massachusetts Institute of Technology for the fall semester. MIT, however, denied Amelia a scholarship, blocking her academic plans and crushing her hopes. She was broke, at a dead end, with no clear direction or path.

Sam Chapman, however, proposed a solution. He had followed her back to Massachusetts and landed a chemical research job with the Boston Edison Company. Sam wanted to wed and support Amelia in a traditional marriage, but even in her most discouraged moments, she had no intention of giving up her independence. "I don't want to marry him. I don't want to marry anyone," she said to Marian Stabler. Sam even offered to change jobs, thinking his demanding schedule was Amelia's biggest objection, but his offer only alienated her further. "I don't want to tell Sam what he should do," she complained to Muriel. "He ought to know what makes him happiest, and then do

By her late twenties, Amelia had found fame in the sky but was battling dispiriting illness and financial problems.

it, no matter what other people say. I know what I want to do, and I expect to do it," she insisted, "married or single."

In truth, however, for the time being Amelia had "no special plan" for herself, except to scratch together some kind of a living. To do so, she started taking on part-time teaching jobs in the Boston area—tutoring blind students in trigonometry and teaching English to foreigners, through the State Board of Education's university extension department. Her class schedule was grueling; she had to travel from Medford to other outlying suburbs of Boston, with little pay or reimbursement for gasoline. As a more efficient, less taxing alternative, she came up with her own plan and taught English at a

business that hired a large number of immigrants. Before long, however, Amelia grew bored with that arrangement and decided to quit. Searching widely for income and inspiration, she even took a job as a nurse-companion at a private residential hospital for mentally ill patients. But the position was low-paying and menial, with no independence or hope of advancement, and she quit that, too, after a few months. Only two years before, she had been flying high above trouble in her yellow plane, with nothing but blue skies and adventure on the horizon. Now she was stuck in a deep rut, with nowhere to go. She was stalling out.

3
TAKING OFF

Air mania swept America in 1927. On May 20, lanky twenty-four-year-old Charles Lindbergh climbed into his cramped monoplane at New York's Roosevelt Field and flew solo, nonstop, to Paris over the Atlantic Ocean. His thirty-three-and-a-half-hour odyssey broke barriers of human endurance and possibility. Others had crossed the ocean by air before, but no one had ever done it alone. With less than three hours' sleep before takeoff, Lindbergh battled fog, ice, darkness, and crushing fatigue, holding his eyelids open with his thumbs as he hurtled toward dawn and the French coast.

In a thrill-seeking age of dance marathons, flagpole sitters, and wing-walking carnival pilots, Lindbergh was a risk-taker of a different sort. Modest, direct, youthful, and shy, he was focused instead of flamboyant, a down-to-earth hero in a heady time.

The result was explosive. In France, a hundred thousand people, many waiting six or seven hours, swarmed him when he landed at Le Bourget field. In New York, three weeks later, four million people jammed the route of his ticker tape parade, the greatest reception in the city's history for a private citizen. In Boston, on July 22, the largest throngs ever recorded cheered frantically as he soared overhead in the flashing silver *Spirit of St. Louis*. The crush in the streets was so great that more than a hundred people had to be treated for injuries.

Amelia, still living in Boston, was aware of the import of Lindbergh's historic flight, but she made no comment about it. She was busy and happy;

Opposite Amelia, with the *Friendship* in 1928

Below In 1927, aviator Charles Lindbergh became the first person to fly solo across the Atlantic Ocean in his airplane, the *Spirit of St. Louis.*

Above Lindbergh in the *Spirit of St. Louis,* 1927

finally, it seemed, she had found her calling. For nine months, she had been working in a crowded community center, Denison House, as a part-time social worker—running English classes for adults, organizing games and activities for children, and doing home visits and casework in a rundown neighborhood of Syrian, Chinese, Irish, and Italian immigrants. In October 1926, when she first applied for the job, Marion Perkins, the center's director, had been struck by the charm of the "tall, slender, boyish-looking" young woman, her quiet sense of humor, and the frank, direct look in her grey eyes. Amelia had no special training in social work, but Perkins hired the twenty-nine-year-old, half-time, for $60 a month. She took to her new responsibilities right away. It was a privilege, in her eyes, to get to know the neighborhood "chronics"—to climb dim tenement stairways and visit their homes, sometimes staying for meals, and to help as a friend, she reported, "Mrs. S. and her drunken husband, Mrs. F.'s struggle to get her husband here, Mrs. Z.'s to get her papers in the face of odds."

With her battered old yellow Kissel, which she loved "like a pet dog," Amelia was also making an impression. She let her young Denison House charges climb all over the car—dubbed the "Yellow Peril"—and she'd pile in as many as ten at a time, on the seats and the running boards, for slow-moving jaunts around the block. Often, she'd pack the

Her roadster, which she called the "Yellow Peril," was a magnet for Denison House youngsters.

car with teenage girls and drive them out to the house she shared with Amy and Muriel—for picnics in the yard, her sister remembered, "or for storytelling and marshmallow roasts around the living room fireplace." Amelia also ferried sick neighborhood children to Massachusetts General Hospital and, three times a week, shuttled a small boy—who had been blinded in a kerosene heater explosion—to the Perkins Institute for the Blind, where she was volunteering as a reader and drama teacher.

Amelia was still teaching English to foreign university students, and she was indulging her old fascination with medicine. Her Columbia friend Louise de Schweinitz—who had gone on to earn a medical degree at Johns Hopkins—was working in a Boston hospital, and Amelia talked her way in, posing as a visiting intern, to watch a woman give birth and help Louise treat a carbuncle on a patient's neck. In her off hours, she was also spending a great deal of time with Sam Chapman—driving out to the beach, exploring Boston, and spending hours listening to her extensive collection of gramophone records. Sam,

however, resented the time Amelia was spending with dozens of Syrian, Irish, and Chinese children, when they could be married and starting a family of their own. He was making good money and ready to support a wife and children—but the more he pressed Amelia to marry, the more she resisted, unable to stomach the prospect of life as "a domestic robot."

She was, instead, rediscovering her more adventurous passions. She was going out horseback riding on Sunday mornings, and the wilder the horse and the weather, the happier she was. Amelia started flying again too. She had joined Boston's chapter of the National Aeronautic Association when she first moved to Medford, and in May, she agreed to fly over the city—as a passenger in a plane owned by the Harvard Flying Club—to drop leaflets publicizing a carnival benefiting Denison House. Suddenly, she was back in the public eye. Local newspapers ran photos of her in her helmet, goggles, and full flying regalia, lauding her as one of the few licensed women flyers in the country.

She was also starting to play a new official leadership role in aviation. Amelia had scraped

Special 1927 stamp commemorating Lindbergh's flight from New York to Paris

crossing. Twenty-five hundred people showed up at the airport's opening on July 2, twenty days before the *Spirit of St. Louis* touched down in Boston. Amelia's newsworthiness as a "teacher, social worker, sportsman, and airplane pilot"—and the only woman flyer on the airport's staff—again made her the focus of press attention. This time, she used it to encourage other women to try flying. The involvement of women in aviation, in fact, was very much on Amelia's mind. In September, she dashed off a letter to Ruth Nichols, who had broken her altitude record six years earlier, asking her advice on "forming an organization composed of women who fly." Amelia wasn't a feminist, she explained, but "[I] do rather

That year, Amelia wrote to Ruth Nichols—a record-setting aviator known as "The Flying Debutante"—with the idea of launching a new organization for women pilots.

together a little money to invest in a new airport being built by a young architect named Harold T. Dennison (no relation to Denison House) in the town of Atlantic, outside of Boston. She became one of five incorporators of the new Dennison Airport and personally decorated and furnished the main hangar, sewing the window curtains and selecting the color scheme for the airport office. Like many new airfields around the country, Dennison opened in the summer of 1927 in time for Lindbergh's seventy-five-city aerial tour celebrating his Atlantic

enjoy seeing women tackling all kinds of new problems—new for them, that is."

At Dennison Airport, Amelia was also taking and starting to teach flying lessons and demonstrating a new five-cylinder plane built by Bert Kinner's aviation company. Kinner had introduced her to Harold Dennison, and months later, when Kinner flew his new, improved Airster from L.A. to Boston, he offered Amelia the chance to fly the new plane as much as she wanted, if she would serve as his sales rep and demonstrate the

DENNISON AIRCRAFT CORPORATION
ATLANTIC, MASS.

FLYING STUDENT INSTRUCTION CONTRACT

I, _Amelia M Earhart_ of _West Medford_ Date _Oct 15 1927_

Name of student   Address

hereby represent myself as physically and mentally fit and competent to become an airplane pilot, and I hereby enroll as a flying student of the Dennison Aircraft Corporation. In consideration of the Dennison Aircraft Corporation accepting me as a student, I hereby assume all risks and liability of whatever nature which may arise during the period of my instruction, and release and waive any claim which I may have against said Corporation for any accident or injury to myself arising out of any cause or manner whatsoever, and I agree to indemnify and hold harmless the Dennison Aircraft Corporation against any and all claims for loss or damages which may be made against said Corporation by any third person by reason of any act of mine while I am a student as aforesaid. I further agree to observe all the rules, regulations and instructions of said Dennison Aircraft Corporation, and all instructions of its officers and representatives while I am a student as aforesaid. $20 per hour.

I agree to pay to said Dennison Aircraft Corporation the sum of ~~Two Hundred Fifty (250) Dollars~~ for said flying instruction ~~as follows: One Hundred (100) Dollars in advance for the first three hours of said instruction, and the sum of One Hundred Fifty (150) Dollars in advance for the remaining seven hours of such instruction.~~

It is understood that the entire agreement between the student and the Corporation is contained in this contract, and no officer or employee of the Corporation has the right to vary the terms hereof.

Amelia M. Earhart

Signature of student

In case the student is under 21 years of age, the following clause MUST be signed by his parent or legal guardian:

In consideration of the foregoing, I, the undersigned parent or guardian of said

Name of student

hereby agree and consent to the foregoing contract, and agree to waive and to release and save harmless said Dennison Aircraft Corporation from any and all injuries and damages to said student while engaged in said flying instruction.

Signature of parent or guardian

The Dennison Aircraft Corporation, relying upon the releases and waivers hereinbefore set forth, accepts this student upon the conditions above mentioned.

DENNISON AIRCRAFT CORPORATION

By _Harold Dennison Pres_

PAYMENTS

Amt. of Payments	Date	Flying Time	Date
$ 175.58	192_	hrs.	192_
$	192_	hrs.	192_
$	192_	hrs.	192_
$	192_	hrs.	192_
$	192_	hrs.	192_
		hrs.	192_

Flying Time	Date		
35 M hrs.	35 1	192_	hrs. 192_
45 M hrs.	30 M	192_	hrs. 192_
50 M hrs.		192_	hrs. 192_
30 M hrs.		192_	hrs. 192_
30 M hrs.		192_	hrs. 192_
20 M hrs.		192_	hrs. 192_
hrs.		192_	hrs. 192_

'TAKE TO AIR," WOMAN FLIER URGES HER SEX

AMELIA EARHART

Miss Earhart Surprised That More Do Not Make Use of Planes

Miss Amelia Earhart, teacher, social worker, sportswoman and airplane pilot, paused in her duties at Denison House, 93 Tyler street, yesterday, long enough to express wonderment that other New England women do not take to the air for recreation.

"New England has some of the best yachtswomen and sportswomen in the world," she declared. "I am surprised that more New England women have not gone into flying as a sport. Why is it?"

Her interviewer, having a great fond-

Right In 1927, she became an incorporator of Boston's new Dennison Airport, where she took flying lessons, worked as an instructor, and even decorated the hangar and sewed window curtains for the office.

Far right She was also making headlines again and encouraging other women to try flying.

plane to potential customers. It was a smart move, Kinner knew, for a woman to show his plane—it would draw attention, and customers typically assumed that if a woman was doing the flying, it must be easy.

With a plane at her disposal, Amelia now "went upstairs" as much as she could. On clear Sundays, she would pick up her sister in her yellow roadster and dash out to the airport, where she would throw on her jodhpurs, helmet, and leather jacket

and take off in the new plane. She loved the power, speed, and sheer beauty of being airborne, but she also enjoyed the greasy nuts and bolts of aviation. Local pilots and mechanics, according to Muriel, liked and respected her as a woman who didn't mind getting her hands greasy—"who could not only fly well, but who also knew about engine performance, tensile strengths, and something about instrument flying." She watched, asked questions, and helped service her plane; "she admitted to her lack of experience," Muriel observed, and was eager to learn.

Amelia was, according to Marion Perkins, "an unusual mixture of the artist and the practical person." She was also a writer of "accuracy and originality," Perkins commented, as well as a poet. Amelia, she recalled, had composed a memorable verse one Sunday afternoon that she titled "Courage." It was inspired by a Denison House meeting the week before, where the staff had discussed *The Challenge of Life*—a book by a popular lecturer—and the courage it takes to make hard decisions. Amelia copied out the poem and showed it, at work, to Marion Perkins:

> *Courage is the price that Life exacts for*
> * granting peace.*
> *The soul that knows it not, knows*
> * no release*
> *From little things:*
> *Knows not the livid loneliness of fear,*
> *Nor mountain heights where bitter joy*
> * can hear*
> *The sound of wings.*
> *How can Life grant us boon of*
> * living, compensate*
> *For dull grey ugliness and pregnant hate*
> *Unless we dare*
> *The soul's dominion?*
> *Each time we make a choice, we pay*
> *With courage to behold resistless day,*
> *And count it fair.*

Amelia was making brave decisions in her own life. In the fall of 1927, she made her "declaration of independence" from her family as well as Sam—moving out of her Medford home into an upstairs apartment at Denison House as a full-time resident worker. She was by then a valued member of the settlement house staff. She had a "keen insight into child life," according to Marion Perkins, who put her in charge of pre-kindergarten and girls five to fourteen. With rewarding work, the chance to fly, and outlets for her leadership and creative energies, Amelia was packing the most she could into every day. "She wanted to do so many things," Perkins remembered—writing, teaching, flying, and furthering the interests of women in aviation. Her life had settled into a contented pattern of engaging responsibilities, growing independence, and quiet adventures.

Several months later, early in 1928, Amelia took up her pen again, this time as a magazine writer, to encourage more women to begin flying. With characteristic directness, she walked into the

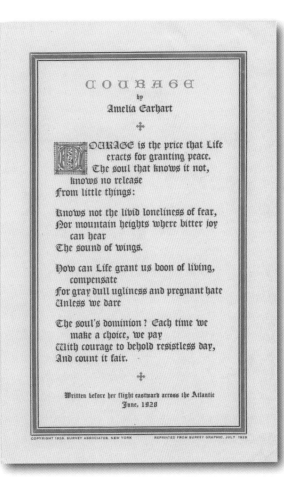

Amelia wrote this poem, "Courage," when she was working at Denison House.

offices of the trend-setting *Bostonian* magazine and offered to write an article about aviation. The tall "curly-headed girl" struck editor Katherine Crosby as "a real thoroughbred." Amelia, she reported, "curled up on the couch in *The Bostonian's* sitting room and wondered if she could write us an article . . . to make flying interesting to women." She had so little vanity, Crosby added, that "I had to persuade her to allow her name to be signed to the article," which was published in May 1928.

Women flyers in those days—pilots as well as passengers—were grabbing headlines. Not only were they curiosities, but they were also risking, and losing, their lives like many men—seeking glory and a place in history, in Lindbergh's wake,

by daringly trying to fly across the Atlantic Ocean. Three months after Lindbergh's flight, the first of four women—including a princess, a movie star, and a millionairess—attempted to be the first to make the Atlantic crossing in an airplane. In Wiltshire, England, on August 31, 1927, sixty-two-year-old Princess Lowenstein-Wertheim—the first woman to fly across the English Channel—climbed into a Fokker airplane with two male pilots and settled into an armchair for what she thought would be a thirty-eight-hour flight over the Atlantic to Ottawa. Her plane disappeared

without a trace, a few hours later, off the Irish coast.

Six weeks later, American flyer Ruth Elder and her co-pilot, George Haldeman, took off from Roosevelt Field in an airplane called *The American Girl* on a 3,600-mile flight to Ireland. Nearly out of gas, they were forced to ditch their plane in the middle of the Atlantic off the Azores, where they were hauled out of the water by a passing tanker. In late December, Mrs. Frances Grayson, a New York real estate millionairess, attempted to fly across the wintry Atlantic from New York to Copenhagen with a crew of three men; heading north, they vanished somewhere off the New England shore. And in March 1928, a thirty-four-year-old pilot and movie star named Elsie Mackay—the

daughter of Britain's Lord Inchcape—took off from an English airfield, bound for the United States. The mystery of her disappearance was only partially solved a few days later, when bits of her plane washed up on the coast of Donegal. All in all, in the twelve months after Lindbergh's historic flight, fifty-five people tried to cross the Atlantic by air. Three women and eleven men perished in the attempt. Only eight flyers in three planes made it safely across—and no woman, so far, had ever succeeded.

The toll of the Atlantic "death lane," however, only seemed to make other women more determined to try. One eager aerial adventuress was Mabel Boll, a flamboyant actress and socialite known as the "Queen of Diamonds." A bartender's

After Lindbergh's Atlantic solo, adventurous women from all walks of life raced to be first to make the deadly crossing of the Atlantic by airplane, including (from left) Princess Lowenstein-Wertheim, who disappeared off the Irish coast; pilot Ruth Elder, who ditched her plane in the middle of the ocean; flyer and movie star Elsie Mackay, who vanished after take-off in England; and real estate mogul Frances Grayson, who perished in the wintry Atlantic.

Right Actress and socialite Mabel Boll, called the "Queen of Diamonds" for her glittering jewels, wanted to be "Queen of the Air" as the first woman to fly across the Atlantic.

Far right
Heiress and adventuress Amy Guest, shown with her son Winston, was determined to find a respectable American woman to cross the Atlantic Ocean in a plane she had purchased for that purpose and named the *Friendship*.

daughter from Rochester, New York, Boll had married into a Colombian coffee fortune in Paris. She sported a 46.57-carat ring, a gift from her husband, and draped herself in dozens of diamond bracelets from shoulder to wrist. Boll's goal, however, was to become "Queen of the Air." In 1927, she had tried unsuccessfully to fly west over the Atlantic in a monoplane piloted by Bert Acosta and Charles A. Levine. In the spring of 1928, she planned to make another try—in order to show off, according to *Time* magazine, her new "Parisian sweater woven from gold links."

This was all too much for another, more socially respectable American adventuress named Amy Guest. A Pittsburgh heiress and the daughter of Henry Phipps, Andrew Carnegie's partner, she was married to Frederick Guest, former Air Minister of Britain. Mrs. Guest was a woman of "terrifying energy" with an interest in adventure

and aviation, and she came up with her own transatlantic scheme. Since she had to be in London in early June for her daughter's presentation at court, she decided to travel in a seaplane, called the *Friendship,* across the Atlantic. As a gesture of amity between Britain and America, she planned to land it in the Thames in front of the Houses of Parliament. Guest kept her plan a secret from her family—revealing it only to her brother Howard and the Phipps family's lawyer, David Layman, whose help she needed to secure an airplane. She asked Layman to persuade Commander Richard E. Byrd—the famous Arctic explorer, based in Boston—to sell her his Fokker trimotor. Byrd agreed, and with his help she also lined up a seasoned pilot, Wilmer Stultz—even though Stultz had already promised to fly Mabel Boll.

The scheme rapidly unraveled, however, when Howard Phipps leaked the plan to Guest's eldest son, Winston Frederick, who was studying law. Winston complained that he would be taking his exams during his mother's flight, and that it would be impossible for him to concentrate under the circumstances. The rest of the family took Winston's side, and Guest ultimately gave in—but not altogether. She still had the use of Commander Byrd's plane, and she was determined that "a suitable American woman" would fly across the Atlantic in her place. To find this exemplary female, Guest turned, once again, to David Layman. He was trying to figure out just how to do that when the solution "dropped from the clouds" in the person of George Palmer Putnam.

G. P., as he was known, was a man with a "dangerous combination" of literary ability, business sense, energy, and determination who had grown up in one of America's great publishing families. His grandfather had founded G. P. Putnam's Sons, a venerable house linked to such literary icons as Washington Irving, Edgar Allen Poe, Nathaniel Hawthorne, and James Fenimore Cooper. G. P., too, had pursued a career in publishing, but he was more drawn to the business of adventure. The biggest adventure figure of the day was Richard Byrd, and G. P. had recently published Byrd's first book, *Skyward*, which chronicled his expedition to Antarctica and flight to the North Pole. G. P. had also created a sensation by publishing Lindbergh's bestselling book, *We*, only two months after the flyer's return to the United States.

G. P. practiced what he published. In 1926, he had led his own expedition to the Arctic and the west coast of Greenland, sponsored by the American Museum of Natural History, and in 1927 he had voyaged to Baffin Island to collect wildlife specimens for the American Geographical Society. In the course of these exploits, of course,

books often resulted, feeding his publishing enterprise. As a result, when this "ubiquitous, omniferous, Publisher-Explorer-Publicist," as *Time* described him, appeared in Layman's New York office in April 1928, it was no accident. While he was riding a ferry to Staten Island, he had gotten wind, by chance, that Guest had bought Byrd's plane. Later that day, he asked his friend Captain Hilton Railey, who was visiting from Boston, to check out the rumor. "If it's true," G. P. told him, "we'll crash the gate . . . Find out all you can. Locate the ship. Pump the pilots . . . Telephone me if it's hot." Before midnight, Railey had returned home to Boston, where he located Wilmer Stultz and his co-pilot and mechanic, Lou Gordon, at the

Publisher, publicist, and adventurer George Palmer Putnam, known as G. P., offered to help Guest find "the right sort of girl."

Above Amelia was considered a suitable young woman for the *Friendship* flight, and many thought she had a striking resemblance to Charles Lindbergh (opposite page).

Copley Plaza hotel. Stultz had been drinking and revealed that he was, indeed, getting ready for an Atlantic flight, and the man who knew all about it, he disclosed, was David Layman.

Armed with this information, G. P. paid Layman a visit, mentioning that he was seasoned in the business of aviation projects and expeditions. Layman, looking "visibly relieved," asked for G. P.'s help in finding "the right sort of girl" to fly across the Atlantic Ocean. There were, he added, some specifications. She should be college-educated, with a pleasing appearance and good manners, and she should know how to fly. The project, G. P. thought, "smacked of zesty adventure," and managing it, he reckoned, would be amusing. "Just then," G. P. recalled, "my career as a publisher of

exploration and adventure books was in full cry. And here I had stumbled on an adventure-in-the-making which, once completed, certainly should provide a book."

G. P. asked Railey to help him find a suitable young aviator to fly the Atlantic. On a hunch, Railey telephoned a friend, a retired rear admiral, who stated that he knew "a young social worker who flies"—a "thoroughly fine" person, he added, who was deeply interested in aviation. Railey would be able to find her at Denison House.

For Amelia Earhart, the unexpected, as she put it, became the inevitable. On an afternoon in April, as children were swarming into Denison House after school, she was busy steering them to classes and activities and making sure

that game leaders and teachers were all present and ready. In the middle of all the commotion, a youngster came up to her, saying she was wanted on the telephone. Amelia said she was too busy, and that whoever it was should phone back later. The caller, the child insisted, said it was important, so Amelia dropped what she was doing and reluctantly went over to the phone. On the line, she heard a male voice introducing himself as Hilton Railey and asking her, enigmatically, if she would like to participate in "an important but hazardous flight." At first, Amelia thought it was a joke—and said so—but the frank admission of risk, she later said, thrilled her beyond words. She demanded Railey's personal references and, after carefully checking them, made an appointment

to see him that same evening, accompanied by Marion Perkins.

Railey's first impression of Amelia was her amazing resemblance to Charles Lindbergh. When he asked her to take off her hat, she complied, tossing her unruly curls—and the words "Lady Lindy!" flashed through his mind. Her poise, warmth, and dignity, he recalled, convinced him right away that she had the personal traits Layman was looking for. He asked her if she would like to fly the Atlantic and explained the secret project in some detail. "It would sound more exciting," Amelia recalled, if she had been "shockingly frightened," but that wasn't the case; she was drawn to the danger and would never have been able to refuse "such a shining adventure." Amelia wanted to move

The *Friendship*, a Fokker trimotor, was equipped with pontoons in case it was forced down over the ocean.

forward—and her next test would be interviews in New York with G. P., Layman, and John Phipps, the brother of Amy Guest.

A few days later, Amelia took the train to New York for the meetings, staying with her friend Marian Stabler. She never revealed to her family or Marian what the trip was about—it was all, she was told, to be kept completely secret. During Amelia's interview with Layman and Phipps, she answered questions for more than an hour about her work, activities, hobbies, and education. The men listened carefully to her speech patterns—to detect if she used the word "ain't" or dropped her "gs"—but they weren't particularly interested

in her flying skills. They explained to Amelia that she would be crossing the Atlantic as a passenger, not a pilot; Stultz would be at the controls, and Lou Gordon would go with them as the flight's mechanic. Although the men would be paid, they explained—Stultz $20,000 and Gordon $5,000—Amelia would receive no compensation. She agreed anyway. Although she hated the idea of just going along as "extra weight," she lacked experience in instrument flying, and "the privilege of being included in the expedition," she believed, was payment enough.

Of the three men she met in New York, G. P. especially impressed Amelia; he was "a fascinating man," she confided to Marion Perkins when she got back to Boston. Six foot two and "very handsome," he had "snapping dark eyes and close-cropped hair," an acquaintance remembered, "and you could feel his electricity across a room." He was also "irascible, sly, opinionated, a total stranger to fear," another observed—"gifted (or cursed) with a vinegar wit," and "the champion of raw charm," although brusque and not particularly gallant. He had taken Amelia to the train station in a taxi, but "once he got me to the station," she complained to Perkins, "he hustled me aboard the Boston train like a sack of potatoes," never even offering to pay her fare.

Next came days of waiting; Amelia had no idea whether she was going, or even if the project was still on. G. P. and Railey had asked her, meanwhile, to "clear the decks" so she would be able to leave at a moment's notice. That wasn't easy. The Denison House staff was starting to make plans for the summer, and Amelia was supposed to direct the summer school. She would have to work quietly with Marion Perkins to find a replacement, while keeping the project a secret from the rest of the staff. Meanwhile, Amelia relaxed, when she had time, by flying over the New England beaches and marshes. Other aviation affairs, too, were keeping her busy. She had written to the Boston chapter of the NAA, raising the notion of creating a separate organization for women; they responded by nominating Amelia to be vice president, the first female officer in the chapter's history. She was also asked to judge a model airplane contest sponsored by the National Playground Association—activities that were "sheer fun," she said, and connected to flying.

Since she was well known around the Boston airfields, she was careful to keep far away from the *Friendship*. The first time Amelia saw the

plane, it was jacked up in a hangar in East Boston, surrounded by mechanics and welders. Its gold-painted wings spanned seventy-two feet, and its fuselage was painted a bright reddish orange, since "a little bright spot bobbing about on the water" had the best chance of attracting attention.

Stultz and Gordon were busy getting the plane ready—taking it for test flights and checking its performance, engines, instruments, carrying capacity, and speed. The Fokker trimotor was being equipped, the public assumed, for Byrd's upcoming expedition to the South Pole, since preparations for the Atlantic crossing were kept strictly secret. Byrd himself was now serving as the team's technical adviser, and he brought on a fourth crew member, Lou Gower, to serve as relief pilot. The *Friendship* would no longer be making a water landing, since Guest's original plan to land it in the Thames River had been scrapped by British officials. The new plan was to fly the *Friendship* to Newfoundland, where it would refuel, then head for Southampton

To keep the planned flight a secret, word was spread that the plane was being readied for Commander Byrd's upcoming expedition to the South Pole.

CONQUERING THE ANTARCTIC *with* BYRD

from Trepassey Harbor on the easternmost Avalon Peninsula, trimming the crossing distance to eighteen hundred miles. The Fokker land plane, however, was still being fitted with huge pontoons, at

Despite the dangers of the flight, Amelia jumped at the adventure and wrote "popping off" letters to her parents in case she didn't survive.

Byrd's insistence, as a safety measure in case the crew ran into trouble over water.

Finally, Amelia was told that the flight would be going; not only was she invited to be on it, she was also officially to be named commander, since the presence of a woman was the sole purpose of the *Friendship*'s flight. Amelia "couldn't say no" to the opportunity. She knew there was danger and the real possibility of death, but "when a great adventure's offered you—you don't refuse it," she told Railey's wife, Julia, who urged her to consider backing out.

Instead, Amelia wrote out a will, directing that her meager assets—one bond, the Yellow Peril, and a few shares of Dennison Airport and Kinner stock—should be sold to pay off her debts, which totaled over $1,000. Anything left, she directed, should go to her mother. Amelia also wrote two "popping off letters," one to each parent, in case she didn't return. To Edwin, she wrote: "Dearest Dad: Hooray for the last grand adventure! I wish I had won, but it was worth while anyway. You know that I have no faith we'll meet anywhere again but I wish we might. Anyway, good-by and good luck to you. Affectionately, your doter, 'Mill.'" To Amy, Amelia wrote: "Even though I have lost, the adventure was worth while. Our family tends to be too secure. My life has really been very happy, and I didn't mind contemplating its end in the midst of it." Amelia's statement that her family was "too secure" is remarkable, given the history of alcoholism, separation, divorce, and poverty she had struggled through; it was a sign of how little she liked to acknowledge conflict and how much she naturally tried to mask sorrow and pain.

G. P., meanwhile, was back in New York, relishing his new role as the adventure's "producer." One morning in early May—when his wife, Dorothy, was driving him to the train station in their hometown of Rye, New York—he confided to her that he was involved in a secret project that could be as sensational, from a publishing perspective, as Lindbergh's *We.* A week or so later, he came home so animated about the project that Dorothy, finally hearing the details, thought it might be the biggest, most ambitious undertaking of his career.

G. P.'s passion for the exploit was growing daily—but there was little, anymore, in his seventeen-year marriage to Dorothy. Heiress to the Crayola crayon fortune, Dorothy Binney had married G. P. in 1911 when she was twenty-three.

Together, they had shared years of adventure—living for a period in Bend, Oregon, where G. P. published the *Bend Bulletin* and served as mayor; traveling through Europe on publishing business; joining geographic expeditions; and producing two sons, David and George Junior, nicknamed "Junie." By 1927, however, their marriage had started going cold. G. P. was spending more and more time away, and Dorothy was discovering that she liked the separation. "Soon we'll see each other by appointment only," she recorded in her diary that year. "Well it suits me . . . " She could no longer even bring herself to have a physical relationship with her husband. For a year now,

G. P. started molding Amelia's image in Boston before she took off in the *Friendship.*

however, she had been happily rediscovering her "gay, intense, utterly pagan self" in the arms of a handsome young Yale undergraduate named George Weymouth, whom G. P. had asked to move into their home as their sons' tutor. A month after Dorothy started her affair with Weymouth, she was putting away G. P.'s summer clothes when she found a compromising letter to her husband from a woman whose name she didn't know. Instead of feeling jealous, Dorothy confided to her diary, she was relieved.

Now, in late May 1928, G. P. was away again, staying in Boston. Amelia had moved into the Copley Plaza—registered, oddly, under the name "Dorothy Binney"—and G. P. arranged for a news photographer, Jake Coolidge, to shoot exclusive pictures of her—in her brown breeches, leather coat, high-laced boots, helmet, and goggles—on the hotel's roof, for future release. Coolidge personally saw little resemblance between Amelia and Lindbergh, but he deliberately made it "seem to be there," he explained, "by camera angles." G. P. was constantly with Amelia and raved to his wife about her grace, intelligence, and warm sense of humor—although he was, according to a friend, not so much smitten with Amelia as "romancing a property."

G. P. had originally hoped the *Friendship* would take off from Boston on May 20, on the one-year anniversary of Lindbergh's flight, but bad weather had dragged on for weeks, delaying plans. Thinking it would be helpful for Amelia to have a female companion during the wait, he called Dorothy and asked her to come up to Boston. Dorothy, for her part, was eager to meet G. P.'s "girl flyer," whose nerve and courage she really admired. At thirty-nine, Dorothy, like Amelia, was fearless and "addicted to risk." She was strong, tall, and athletic—a champion swimmer—and she and Amelia both favored cropped hair and loose, flowing clothes. The two became fast friends and spent six days almost always together, passing time—with G. P., the Stultzes, the Gowers, Gordon and his fiancée, and occasionally the Laymans—going to the theater and restaurants and sightseeing in the Yellow Peril. One early morning, in the darkness before dawn, Amelia and Dorothy parked the car near the harbor; Amelia cuddled up in Dorothy's coat, and they sat for hours, "talking and grinning" and watching the *Friendship* bobbing on the swells.

Dorothy returned to Rye on May 28—and finally, five days later, there was a break in the weather. On June 3, after three scuttled takeoff attempts, the crew and a small group of well-wishers left the Copley Plaza before dawn, stopping for breakfast at an all-night restaurant, and headed through deserted streets to T Wharf, where they boarded a tugboat called the *Sadie Ross*. When it arrived at the *Friendship*, moored off the Jeffrey Yacht Club in East Boston, Stultz, Gordon, Gower, and Amelia climbed in, and the seaplane started taxiing down the harbor. Stultz headed the big orange plane into the wind, but the drag of the heavy pontoons kept them glued to the surface. They tried four more times, again and again, but still the water wouldn't release them. To lighten the plane, they dumped out six of their eight five-gallon cans of gasoline, and Gower, on his own initiative, jumped out of the plane onto the tug. For the first time, finally, Amelia felt the *Friendship* lighten on the water; the difference of a few pounds "made her a bird." It was a scary takeoff, though—the cabin door suddenly flew open just after they started climbing, and she and Gordon came within inches of falling out.

As the *Friendship* headed toward Canada, Amelia settled herself, uncomfortably, on the floor of the unheated cabin. There was no passenger

Opposite G. P. started promoting her as "Lady Lindy" and commissioned photos that would play up her resemblance to Lindbergh.

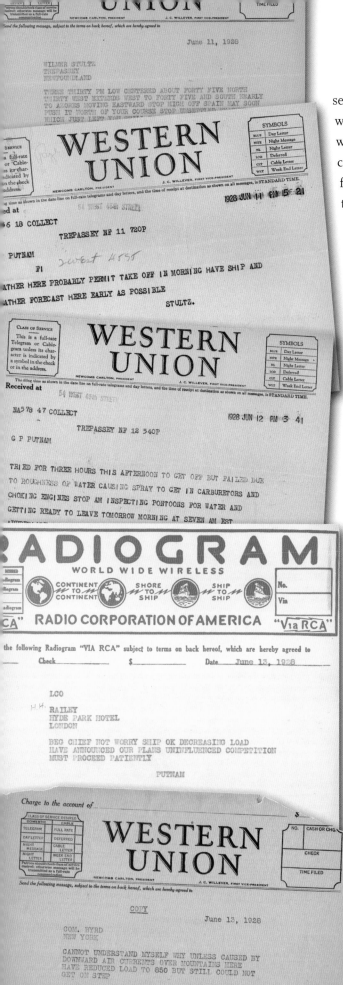

seating in the *Friendship*, which was crammed with two large elliptical tanks filled with fuel, a small table for the navigation instruments, rolled-up flying suits, and a five-gallon can of water. Amelia spent most of her time wedged between the tanks, where she could feel a little warmth from the cockpit heater. She mainly had with her what she wore—the same gear she had posed in for the photographs, with a white silk blouse, red necktie, and brown sweater. In a small army knapsack she had a toothbrush, a comb, and some cold cream and handkerchiefs. Beyond that, she had a borrowed fur-lined flying suit, camera, watch, field glasses, and a leather-bound journal G. P. had given her, inscribed with the words: "A. E. FROM G. P. 5/15/28."

The crew planned to fly directly to Trepassey, where they would spend two or three days and refuel before heading out across the Atlantic Ocean. Due to bad weather conditions, however, they were forced to stop for a night in Halifax, where reporters were already on their heels. When they at last got to Trepassey, the crew ran into more trouble. Day after day of weather and mechanical problems kept them pinned down, "on the ragged edge" of stress and frustration, for two more weeks. The strain of those endless days, Amelia wrote, was the most taxing experience she had ever had, mainly because Stultz had started drinking heavily. Amelia and Gordon tried to distract him by taking him out hiking and fishing, but Stultz would pull a bottle out of his pocket or find any excuse to go back to town. It got so bad that Amelia, as commander, seriously considered replacing him with Gower. But she had more faith in Stultz's skills as a pilot, and she stuck with him.

Adding to the pressure was news that Mabel Boll—outraged that Stultz had abandoned her for the *Friendship* flight—had recruited two World War I flying aces to pilot her plane up to Newfoundland, where she, too, was waiting to set out over the Atlantic. In London, Amy Guest denied that the *Friendship* would ever engage in a race with Mabel Boll. But Amelia was feeling the stress; to distract her, G. P. wired the suggestion that she "think of fresh wardrobe in London and grin." He also recommended that, to keep busy, she start writing a skeleton thousand-word sketch on the progress of the *Friendship*, with names, places, and details that she could expand on later.

In one ten-day period, the dispirited crew made a dozen attempts to take off from the narrow harbor; time after time, they were cemented to the water by the huge pontoons. By the night of June 16, Amelia was at the end of her rope.

She and Gordon were playing cards; Stultz had been drinking and was stumbling and cursing in his room overhead. Finally, at 11 p.m., Amelia received a cable stating that the weather was looking clear for the next forty-eight hours. She decided right then that they would take off after daylight, even though Stultz seemed to be utterly unfit to fly. In the morning, with Gordon's help, she was able to rouse him with hot coffee and splashes of cold water, and they practically dragged him down the steep path to the airplane. It was, G. P. commented, "the bravest or silliest act of her whole career." Amelia felt certain that Stultz's flying instinct would kick in once they were airborne, and she had to take advantage of the moment.

After climbing into the *Friendship*, waves pounding the pontoons, the crew taxied to the end of the harbor and faced into the wind. They had lightened their craft, and shortened their range, by reducing the fuel they carried to seven hundred gallons and eliminating everything they possibly could, including their rubber life raft. Still, the *Friendship* seemed too heavy to rise. Stultz turned the plane around and tried again. This time, they raced down the harbor at such speed that the *Friendship* rocked and staggered dangerously until, finally, it rose into the air.

Aloft at last, Amelia settled down and was about to start making notes in her log when she spotted a whiskey bottle, three-quarters full, that Stultz had stashed secretly behind his tool bag. Amelia's first impulse was to throw it out of the plane, through the trap door in the bottom of the fuselage. But she thought better of it—perhaps remembering, years before, how her father had nearly struck her, enraged, after she'd emptied his whiskey bottle down the kitchen sink. In the end, Amelia opted to leave Stultz's bottle where it

was, hoping he would never think to come back and get it.

They were flying, finally, over the Atlantic Ocean, but they hardly ever saw the sea stretching below. Despite the promise of fine weather, it was "a voyage in the clouds," Amelia wrote, through almost constant banks of fog, rain, and even snow. All three of them were so distracted that they hardly ate. In twenty hours, Amelia drank nothing and only swallowed six malted milk tablets and three oranges. She was too busy writing in her log book, talking to Gordon and Stultz, and "getting housemaid's knee" kneeling beside the chart table, "gulping beauty" through the port-side window. "At times," she wrote, "we seemed to be flying straight into rings all the colors of the rainbow" and fields blazing with stars.

For Stultz and Gordon, it was a harrowing flight. Since eight o'clock the first evening, they had been flying blind, by instruments alone. The radio was out; with no word from ships below,

Opposite
Telegrams detailing takeoff delays in Trepassey, Newfoundland, that had Amelia "on the ragged edge" of stress and frustration

Above The *Friendship's* crew— (seated from left) pilot Wilmer Stultz, Amelia, and co-pilot Lou Gordon—pose with famous aviators and explorers (standing, from left) Ben Eielson, Hubert Wilkins, Richard Byrd, Clarence Chamberlin, and Bernt Balchen.

Above Amelia
at the door of the
Friendship after
crossing the Atlantic
and landing in Burry
Port, Wales, after a
nearly twenty-one-
hour flight

Opposite bottom
The *Friendship*
travels to Southamp-
ton, England, for its
official welcome

the only way they could check their position was by dead reckoning. Suddenly, they spied a big transatlantic vessel crossing their path, and Amelia wrote a note asking the captain to paint his bearings on the deck. She put it in a bag—with a couple of oranges for ballast—and dropped it through the hatch, aiming for the deck, but the message landed in the water far from the ship. With no real sense of position, the crew kept heading eastward until finally, out of the fog, shadowy, sea-beaten cliffs slowly emerged. Stultz nosed the plane down through the clouds, soaring low over "a story-book country-side" of hedges, fields, and tree-lined roads. Cruising along the shore,

they descended near a little town—the end of the journey, they realized, since they were nearly out of gas. Stultz set the plane down in an estuary, half a mile from shore, and, after fastening the *Friendship* to a buoy, they all waited patiently in a torrential downpour for the local welcome.

It was a long wait. No matter how much they shouted and waved, trying to attract attention, the villagers ignored them. After a while, however, a boatload of constables approached, and Stultz, Gordon, and Amelia explained that they had just come from America. Soon, more boats started coming out, and groups of people—hundreds, then thousands—slowly started gathering in the rain.

The *Friendship* had landed, it turned out, in Burry Port, Wales—a long distance from Southampton, where Hilton Railey and Amy Guest had been waiting to greet them. When Railey got word they had come down safely in south Wales, he chartered a flying boat and, a few hours later, pulled up next to the *Friendship* in the Bristol Channel. There, he remembered, he saw Amelia "seated Indian fashion in the doorway of the fuselage," indifferent to the noisy crowds gathered on shore. "Congratulations!" Railey yelled to her—"how's it feel to be the first woman to fly the Atlantic?" "Hello!" Amelia replied, with a listless wave. "It was a grand experience," she continued, with a disappointed look, but "I was just baggage, like a sack of potatoes . . . Maybe some day," she added, brightening, "I'll try it alone."

The next morning, she finally had a turn at the controls of the *Friendship* for a while when they set off by air down to Southampton. There, as ships blasted their horns and well-wishers crowded the dock, Amelia met Mrs. Guest for the first time, then boarded a yellow Rolls-Royce and headed to London.

Although Amelia was official commander of the flight, Wilmer Stultz piloted the plane, and she was, she said, like baggage, a "sack of potatoes."

WASHINGTON D.C.
June eighteenth.

I wish to express to you, the first woman
successfully to span the North Atlantic by air, the
great admiration of myself and the people of the
United States for your splendid flight.   Our pride
in this accomplishment of our countrywoman is
equalled only by our joy over her safe arrival.
The courageous collaboration of the copilot, Mr.
Wilmer Stultz, and Mr. Gordon, likewise merit our
cordial congratulations.

CALVIN COOLIDGE

Amelia's welcome in the British capital was beyond anything she ever expected. At the Hyde Park Hotel, there were mountains of letters and telegrams, including a message of congratulations from President Coolidge. Her telephone rang constantly,

and she couldn't walk out the door without being practically rushed off her feet by adoring crowds. Amelia, who dreaded tumult and noise, was grateful when Amy Guest offered the sanctuary of her Park Lane home. Amelia moved into the mansion with no luggage, just a toothbrush and the flying togs she was wearing. Faced with a packed schedule of public, high-profile appearances, she needed a wardrobe, and Guest escorted her to Selfridge's for a shopping spree.

In the glare of publicity—receptions, banquets, newsreels, and newspaper articles—Amelia was always quick to credit the success of the *Friendship* flight to Stultz and Gordon, explaining, time after time, that she had just been a passenger. It was Amelia, however, the crowds clamored to see, and she was an instant celebrity. Stultz and Gordon were left to drift by themselves around London, undisturbed and unnoticed by the press. Alone in the spotlight, Railey recalled, Amelia remained "serious, forthright, with no break in her make-up," but she was overwhelmed. The crowds made her nervous, and her only escape from the constant attention was at 5:30 one morning, when

Opposite Amy Guest (second from left) and the lady mayor of Southampton, Mrs. Foster Welch (far right) greet Gordon, Amelia, and Stultz; President Calvin Coolidge sent Amelia his congratulations.

Above Photographers crowding the *Friendship*'s crew

she secretly left the Guest residence and took a taxi to a Croydon airfield. There she went up for two hours in a little airplane, an Avian Moth, owned by Lady Mary Heath, who had recently flown it solo on a ten-thousand-mile record flight from Cape Town to London. On June 26, with money advanced by G. P., Amelia purchased the plane from Lady Heath, who inscribed the fuselage with a special message: "To Amelia Earhart from Mary Heath. Always think with your stick forward."

Two days later, Amelia, Stultz, Gordon, and Railey boarded the SS *President Roosevelt* for the voyage back across the Atlantic to the United States. On July 6, when they sailed into New York Harbor, Dorothy Putnam was on the welcoming boat that went out to meet them, amid sirens and whistles, and was "tickled," she wrote, "to have Amelia throw her arms around me and kiss me, her only kiss, when she stepped aboard." After lunch at the Biltmore, it was on to a ticker tape parade along Broadway and a mayoral reception attended by thousands.

The adulation was repeated in Boston, where hundreds of thousands of well-wishers jammed the financial district in a blizzard of ticker tape and colored streamers. When Amelia did a flyby over Dennison Airport as a passenger in a Ford plane, the pilots and mechanics below shouted and cheered; "great ships in the harbor shrilled their whistles," Dorothy recorded, and "on every roof handkerchiefs waved." Amelia also had time to reconnect, briefly, with family and friends. She had a few moments with Amy and Muriel, visited with children and colleagues from Denison House, and was greeted by Sam Chapman at the Ritz-Carlton hotel when she arrived. A few weeks earlier, Sam had told a reporter that he and Amelia had been engaged since 1924, but Amelia, besieged by inquiries, would not confirm that. "My status so far as any 'engagement' is concerned," she declared in a typewritten statement," is "a purely personal matter and of interest to no one except those directly concerned. Please let us say nothing more about it."

Gradually, it was beginning to dawn on Amelia that she would not be able to return to her old life as she had expected. Before she had set off on the *Friendship* adventure, she had predicted to Marion Perkins that "it won't amount to much." She would soon be back, she was sure, to her routine of "aviation on Sundays and holidays, and social service work the rest of the week." But the realities of her new circumstances were sinking in; her "value as a social worker," she acknowledged to Muriel, "is nil while this hullabaloo keeps up." There was no turning back, at least for now. Amelia was launched.

Opposite Amelia, who thought of herself as "a social worker who flies," returned to Boston in July 1928 as an international star.

4
THE HERO BUSINESS

The rapturous parades and hero's homecomings finally came to an end on July 24, Amelia's thirty-first birthday. She had skyrocketed to fame in a dizzying month, showered with honors and lionized everywhere as a female Lindbergh. Although Amelia, modest and down-to-earth, disliked being a sensational "side show curiosity" and wanted to get back to her private life, G. P., who was now her official manager, had other plans. Instead of returning to Boston and Denison House, Amelia plunged, under his direction, into the high-wire "hero business," striving to profit by—and struggling to preserve—her newfound celebrity.

G. P. had built his career stage-managing high-profile adventurers and publishing first-hand accounts of their dramatic exploits. He wasted no time rushing Amelia's story into print. To make sure she had the space and solitude to write a book on the *Friendship* flight at breakneck speed, he brought her directly to his home in Rye, a comfortable, sprawling Spanish-style house that he and Dorothy called Rocknoll. For six weeks, Amelia lived there as the Putnams' guest, glued to her desk and surrounded by G. P.'s publishing and publicity entourage.

It was "all very hectic and upsetting," Dorothy complained, with large crowds for meals and reporters hovering about, but it was "all in the game," she acknowledged, and she and Amelia, on the surface at least, remained great companions. When Amelia wasn't writing her book or answering the piles of fan letters that poured in—about two hundred a day—she and Dorothy liked to go driving or shopping, and they went swimming together most afternoons. Dorothy adored airplanes, and Amelia took her up in her new little Avian Moth, which had been crated and shipped back to the United States, flying the "small silver darning needle" of a plane in the bracing ocean air off Long Island Sound.

As the days passed, however, there were undercurrents of tension. Dorothy was irked by G. P.'s constant attention to Amelia; they were hardly ever apart—working together in the house, canoeing and

Opposite Amelia, now a high-flying celebrity, christens a plane.

Above A souvenir button celebrating the *Friendship* flight

20 Hrs., 40 Min., she told Dorothy that she wanted to dedicate the book to her. Dorothy was instantly skeptical about Amelia's motives. "Does she really want to?" she wondered in her diary. "Or was it a sop to me because she had monopolized George all summer?" Dorothy wasn't the only one who noticed the growing closeness between G. P. and Amelia. Rumors of a romance were starting to spread, and by August 21, as Dorothy watched them together from afar, she realized that they had suddenly become a couple.

G. P.'s infatuation with Amelia "and his clamor," as Dorothy put it, "to be with her every minute, all day, every day on one pretext or another," began drawing attention. When Amelia finally left Rocknoll at the end of August to realize her years-long dream of "gypsying" across the continent by air, G. P. accompanied her as she set off in the Avian on her way west. He had kept the trip secret from Dorothy and the press, but his presence was embarrassingly revealed in newspaper headlines when Amelia cracked up in Pittsburgh, smashing her landing gear and splintering her propeller after hitting a ditch. To tamp down damaging gossip about an affair, G. P. quickly headed back to Rye while Amelia stayed on in Pittsburgh to deal with reporters and repairs to her plane. He confessed the misadventure to Dorothy, who realized that her husband's "obsession" with Amelia might give her the very excuse she needed for a separation—or perhaps a divorce.

Now on her own, with no plan except to rest and recover from "writer's cramp" on a long, winding aerial vacation, Amelia took off for Los Angeles on September 2, sending telegrams to G. P. at almost every stop. Solitary by nature, she was happy to wander alone in the open skies, following railroads and rivers across Ohio, Indiana, Missouri, New Mexico, and Texas on a two-week trek. To

Just weeks after crossing the Atlantic, Amelia moved into G. P.'s house in Rye, New York, to start writing her first book.

swimming together for hours, and planning the next stage in Amelia's career. Dorothy and G. P. had only a shell of a marriage—she was madly in love with a man nineteen years younger, and "utterly indifferent" to her husband—but G. P. and Amelia were inseparable under her own roof, and she found it galling.

Amelia, for her part, was torn between her friendship with Dorothy and her growing attachment and attraction to G. P. When she completed the first draft of her *Friendship* account, entitled

the press, Amelia called herself "just a dub, flying around the country for personal amusement," but she was also setting new flying records. When she landed in Glendale, California, she became the first woman to fly solo from the Atlantic to the Pacific. She also looked like a "horned toad," she joked, her

to New York on October 13. Buoyed by her Atlantic crossing, book release, and cross-country records, Amelia was a national sensation, and G. P. had engineered a full schedule of commitments to keep her profitably in the public eye. Ray Long, editor-in-chief of *Cosmopolitan*, proudly announced that

Amelia at the beach with G. P.'s wife, Dorothy, and their son David

face brown from exposure except for two white, goggle-shaped rings circling her eyes. In L.A. she visited with Edwin and friends, then headed back east, becoming the first woman to fly the eight-thousand-mile coast-to-coast round trip solo.

She was in the news again—this time as a pilot, not just a "sack of potatoes"—and she was back to work with a vengeance when she returned

she would be the magazine's new aviation editor, writing eight articles a year and fielding readers' questions about flying. Amelia, however, would have scant time to meet her deadlines under G. P.'s management. He scheduled her on a nearly non-stop tour of paid lectures, appearances, receptions, and "chicken and peas" dinners at clubs, colleges, and organizations all across the United States. It was a brutal schedule, and Amelia had to steal time to "sweat out her sentences" in hotels or trains as she dashed from city to city. G. P., for his part, was full of suggestions, telling her not to let her voice drop at the end of sentences, advising her to smile with her lips closed to hide the gap between her

She was busier than ever, writing for *Cosmopolitan* magazine (opposite) and crossing the country on a packed schedule of lectures and appearances.

front teeth, and criticizing the hats she sported as a "cataclysm" and a "public menace."

In November, when G. P. traveled with Amelia for ten days on the lecture circuit, a talented young flyer named Elinor Smith joined the two of them for breakfast one morning in Amelia's Chicago

hotel suite. Elinor was impressed with Amelia's welcoming manner, graciousness, and friendly warmth, and G. P., she recalled, was "wiry and dynamic," had impeccable manners, and "exuded the authority of a bank president." She also picked up an unmistakable intimacy and electricity between them, and it was clear to her that they were sharing the suite's double bed. With rumors continuing to surface, however, G. P. made a point of informing Dorothy that he and Amelia were staying in separate accommodations. It was also beginning to dawn on him that there might be less gossip about the affair so long as he remained married to Dorothy. He had heard "whispers of a 'Putnam break-up' and he's unhappy about that," Dorothy confided to her diary. "He doesn't want us to separate," she wrote, "and feels we're both foolish to let things go too far."

Amelia, meanwhile, was making decisive moves in her own life. On November 22, she publicly announced to the press that she was "no longer engaged to marry," if in fact she ever had been. Her relationship with Sam was over, though they remained close friends, and she had broken the news to him in person a few days earlier. She was also establishing a new residence in New York City. With the money she was making—$500 a week, a substantial sum, on lectures alone—she had stability and independence, but she missed the communal warmth and support of her old life at Denison House. Still viewing herself in some ways as "a social worker who flies," she asked Mary Simkhovitch, director of a Manhattan settlement house, if she could join her staff and live there when she was in town. Mary was happy to oblige, and Amelia, along with Amy, moved into Greenwich House on Barrow Street in the East Village. She felt at home and comfortable there, and her presence was inspiring to those around her. According to Mary's husband,

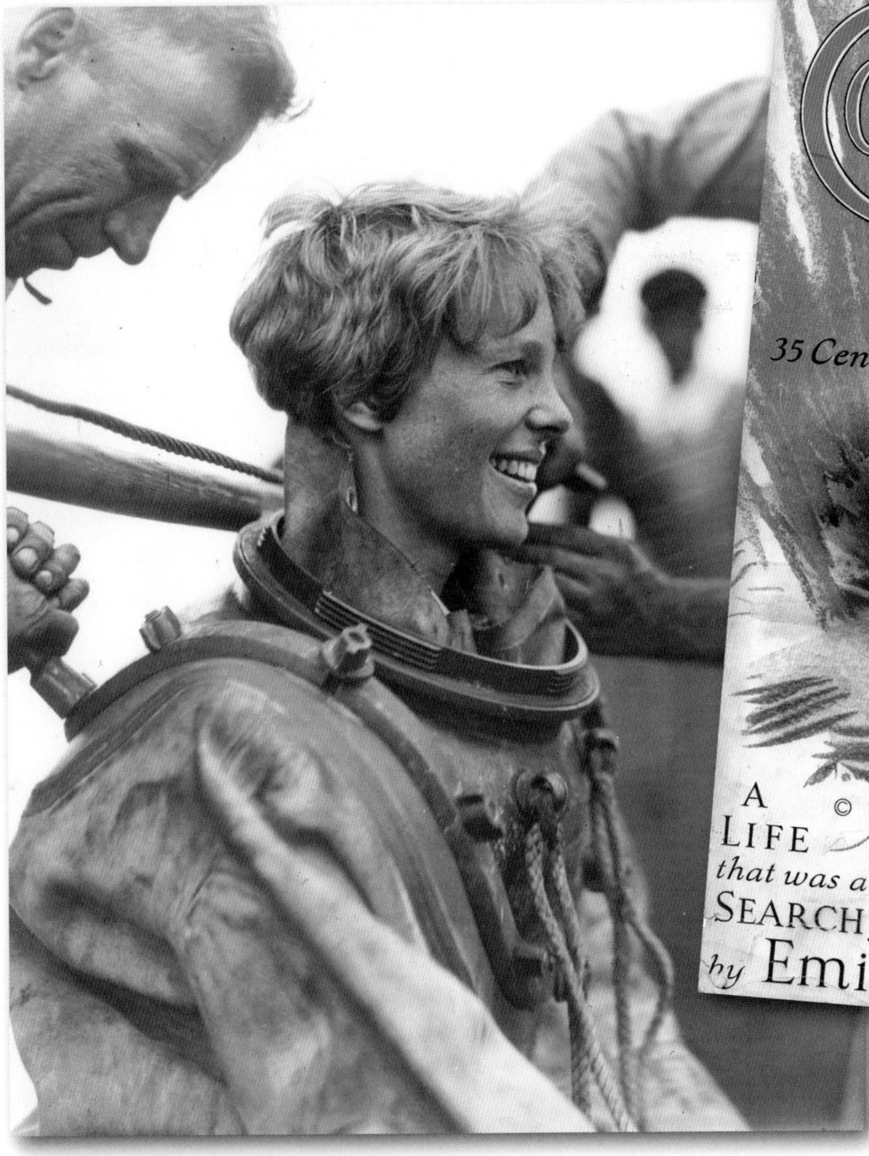

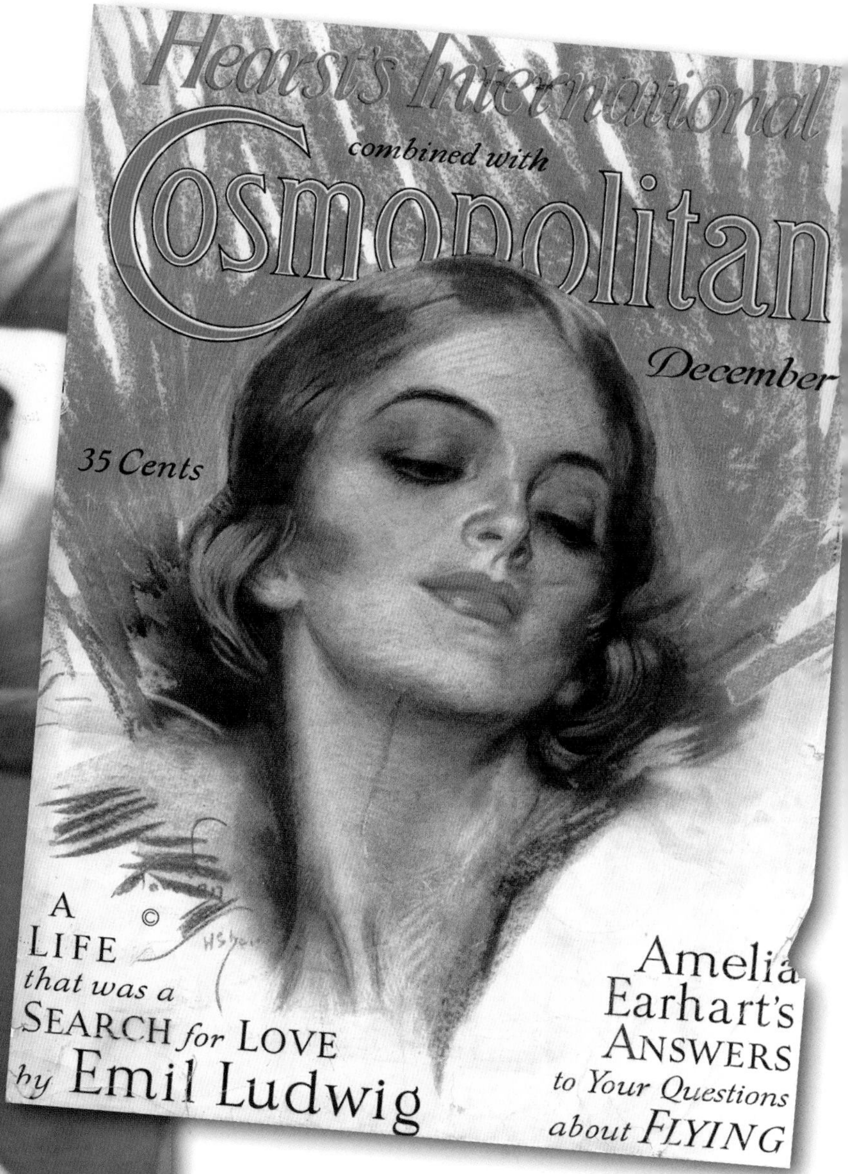
Hearst's International
combined with
Cosmopolitan
December
35 Cents
A LIFE that was a SEARCH for LOVE by Emil Ludwig
Amelia Earhart's ANSWERS to Your Questions about FLYING

a Columbia economist, Amelia was "a thoroughly nice, human, remarkable girl with social as well as moral and ethical conscience, great and poetic sensitivity, and deep feeling for beauty." She also, he recalled, had a burning desire for new sensations, and he worried that "she seemed to have no plan for self-protection," allowing herself to be pushed, perhaps dangerously hard, in the pursuit of money and fame.

But, as Amelia knew, the rule was still "no job, no pay, no fly"; she had to make money, and "the Lady Lindy thing," for now, was the job at hand. She was almost constantly out on the road, traveling to twelve cities in the first half of 1929, speaking to audiences on topics as wide-ranging as the future of aviation, vocational training for girls, even global peace. Amelia liked public speaking and didn't shrink from the limelight; according to Elinor Smith, "the image of a shy and retiring individual thrust against her will into the public eye was a figment of Putnam's lively imagination." Amelia, she later commented, was "about as shy as Muhammad Ali," and the people

Far left In July 1929, Amelia tried underwater diving in a publicity stunt stage-managed by G. P.

who came to see her weren't disappointed. Many expected to find, as G. P. put it, "a massive, mannish individual, big-footed and heavy-handed." Instead, they encountered a graceful, "Peter-Panish" young woman with an intelligent, sensitive face lit by laughter and warmth. Her appealing good looks and down-to-earth charm won audiences over, sometimes overwhelmingly so, and the physical crush of the crowds, which Amelia could scarcely tolerate, worsened the strains of her punishing schedule.

Compounding the stress, her friendship with Dorothy Putnam was falling apart, and even the most common courtesies now seemed unbearably awkward. In January, Dorothy complained that Amelia had never acknowledged her brother's recent death or the gift she'd given her for Christmas, and she was surprised at what seemed to be Amelia's "bad manners." Meanwhile, Dorothy's relations with G. P., too, were reaching a breaking point. He knew she was having an affair with a much younger lover and made cutting, sarcastic remarks about her "interest in kids," but Dorothy was now also involved with another man, a famous World War I flying hero named Frank Upton. Her life with G. P. was disintegrating into rounds of bitter fights, accusations, and nasty encounters. "Why," she wondered, "should we continue to go on this way all our lives? Surely there's some pleasure, peace and joy for us *somewhere*. But not together." In May, Dorothy began packing her things and preparing to move out of Rocknoll. G. P., she wrote a few weeks later, is "fed up, cured, isn't in love with me anymore and is eager, now, for me to go ahead and get a divorce." His haphazard efforts to preserve their marriage seemed to be at an end; it was "odd," Dorothy reflected. "He's got over being in love with me as he called it in about two weeks."

The Putnams' marital discord shadowed Amelia's personal life, but work wise, she had a bright future. On July 1, 1929, she was named assistant to the general traffic manager of one of America's newest commercial airlines, Transcontinental Air Transport (TAT), a company that was offering a novel forty-eight-hour combined air-and-rail service from coast to coast. Amelia's continuing advocacy for women and flying made her an ideal representative for TAT's founder, Clement C. Keyes, who wanted her to focus on the "women's angle" and "the luxuries, refinements and comforts of travel which women demand." Research suggested that men would fly more if their wives felt at ease with commercial airlines, and Amelia's charge was to persuade women that aviation was safe, despite continuing news stories about crashes and flying disasters.

To show women around the country how easy and convenient it was to travel by air, she invited Dorothy, as a gesture of friendship, to join her on TAT's first east-to-west cross-country air-and-rail segments in early July. Despite her ill feelings, Dorothy felt like doing "something dangerous and rash," and she was thrilled to go. Since it was still too treacherous for pilots to fly at night, or through the "hell stretch" of volatile weather over the Alleghenies, she and other TAT passengers traveled by overnight train from New York to Columbus, Ohio, then boarded one of two big three-motor planes that were making the inaugural trips west. She and Amelia traveled on separate airplanes— Dorothy on *The City of Wichita* and Amelia on *The City of Columbus*—to Indianapolis, St. Louis, Kansas City, Wichita, and Waynoka, Oklahoma, where they disembarked and took another overnight train to Clovis, New Mexico. Boarding a second airplane the next morning, passengers flew

Opposite She also helped get a new airline off the ground as assistant to the general traffic manager of Transcontinental Air Transport (TAT), a company that offered combined air-and-rail service across the country.

AIR   RAIL   AIR   RAIL

SAN FRANCISCO · LOS ANGELES · KINGMAN · WINSLOW · ALBUQUERQUE · CLOVIS · WAYNOKA · WICHITA · KANSAS CITY · ST. LOUIS · INDIANAPOLIS · PORT COLUMBUS · CHICAGO · CLEVELAND · PITTSBURGH · PHILADELPHIA · BALTIMORE · WASHINGTON · NEW YORK

COAST TO COAST IN 4[8]

(Daily Through service effective from New York July 7—from Po[...]

The schedule and meal arrangements for the through route between New York, N[...] Francisco, Cal., are given below. Passengers will be ticketed from Pittsburgh, Clevela[...] Railroad on convenient connecting train service to and from Columbus. Tickets [...] any combination of rail and air service included in the through route.

WESTBOUND

Pennsylvania Railroad
THE AIRWAY LIMITED
Eastern Time
Lv. New York (Penna. Sta.), N. Y.* .... 6.05 PM
Lv. North Philadelphia, Pa. 7.50 PM
Lv. Washington, D. C. .... 6.30 PM
Lv. Baltimore, Md........ 7.30 PM
Ar. Port Columbus, O.†... 7.55 AM

Transcont'l Air Transp. Inc.
Lv. Port Columbus, O..... 8.15 AM
Central Time
Ar. Indianapolis, Ind...... 9.13 AM
Lv. Indianapolis, Ind...... 9.28 AM
Ar. St. Louis, Mo........12.03 PM
Lv. St. Louis, Mo.‡......12.18 PM
Ar. Kansas City, Mo...... 2.47 PM
Lv. Kansas City, Mo...... 3.02 PM
Ar. Wichita, Kansas...... 4.56 PM
Lv. Wichita, Kansas...... 5.11 PM
Ar. Airport, Okla. (Landing Field)§............ 6.24 PM
Transfer to Waynoka by Aero Car

San Francisco passengers upon arrival at Los Angeles will be given the option of using overnight trains either from Los Angeles or Glendale, or they may remain overnight in Los Angeles and proceed by Maddux Airline plane morning service from Glendale Airport to San Francisco. Transfers will be provided by aero car between Glendale and the central section of Los Angeles. Tickets for whichever plan is selected by passenger will be furnished by the Transcontinental Air Transport, Inc.

Atch., Topeka & Santa Fe Ry.
Sleeping car ready for occupancy at 8.00 PM
Central Time
Lv. Waynoka, Okla ......11.00 PM
Ar. Clovis, N. M.||........ 8.20 AM
Transfer to Portair by Aero Car

Transcont'l Air Transp. Inc.
Mountain Time
Lv. Portair, N. M. Landing Field .... 8.10 AM
Ar. Albuquerque, N. M....10.17 AM
Lv. Albuquerque, N. M....10.32 AM
Ar. Winslow, Ariz....... 1.12 PM
Lv. Winslow, Ariz.‡...... 1.27 PM
Pacific Time
Ar. Kingman, Ariz........ 2.31 PM
Lv. Kingman, Ariz........ 2.46 PM
Ar. Los Angeles, Cal..... 5.52 PM
(Grand Central Air Terminal, Glendale, Cal. Passengers will be transferred by Aero Car to and from the central section of Los Angeles.)

Transcont'l Air T[...]
Lv. Los Angeles, Cal [...]
(Grand Central A[...] Glendale)
Ar. Kingman, Ariz...[...]
Lv. Kingman, Ariz.‡.[...]

Ar. Winslow, Ariz...[...]
Lv. Winslow, Ariz...[...]
Ar. Albuquerque, N.[...]
Lv. Albuquerque, N.[...]
Ar. Portair, N. M. L[...] Field..........
Transfer to Clovis [...]

Atch., Topeka & [...]
Sleeping car ready [...] at 9.00 [...]

Lv. Clovis, N. M. ..[...]
Ar. Waynoka, Okla [...]
Transfer to Airpo[...]

From San F[...] overnight trains [...] making direct c[...] San Francisco [...] Central Air Te[...] to the central [...] transported by [...]

Dinner and breakfast on Pennsylvania Railroad Dining Car. †A new station stop (Port Columbus) s[...] Fred Harvey Service. §Transfer to Harvey House, Waynoka, Okla., where dinner will be served. ||Breakf[...] querque, Airport—Fred Harvey Service. ®Breakfast at [...]

Apply to any Pennsylvania Railroad agent for full information as to fares, [...]

PENNSYLVANIA R[...]

COAST TO COAST IN 48 HOURS
BY RAIL AND AIR

NEW YORK · CLEVELAND · PORT COLUMBUS · PHILADELPHIA · CHICAGO · PITTSBURGH · INDIANAPOLIS · BALTIMORE · ST. LOUIS · WASHINGTON · KANSAS CITY · WAYNOKA

BY NIGHT....
LUXURIOUS TRAINS
BY DAY......
SAFE SWIFT PLANES

DAILY SERVICE EFFECTIVE FROM NEW YORK JULY 7TH · FROM COLUMBUS JULY 8TH

PENNSYLVANIA RAILROAD
TRANSCONTINENTAL AIR TRANSPORT INC.
ATCHISON · TOPEKA & SANTA FE RAILWAY

Right Amelia (far left, next to Dorothy Putnam), poses with Anne and Charles Lindbergh (far right) after the first coast-to-coast flights on TAT, called the "Lindbergh Line."

Opposite She was regularly flying to appearances in her Avian Moth, a little "cockleshell" of an airplane, like this restored 1927 Avro Avian.

on to Albuquerque, then Winslow and Kingman, Arizona, before finally arriving in Glendale, California. Charles Lindbergh, who was a technical adviser for TAT—known as the "Lindbergh Line"—personally piloted Dorothy's plane for one leg of the trip on July 9. It was an incomparable experience, she recorded; there had been "nothing ever like it before to thrill and excite and enchant me."

The daily reality of TAT flights, however, wasn't quite so glamorous. Amelia publicly admitted that some passengers—"fewer than 5 percent"—suffered from air sickness, but in truth it was a severe and disturbing problem on many planes. According to one pilot, "people were so sick they used rubber matting instead of carpeting on the floor of the plane," and passengers, some said, "skated down the aisle" and "slid out" of the aircraft. Safety, too, was an issue, despite Amelia's soothing reassurance. In September, a TAT plane, *The City of San Francisco,* crashed into a mountain, killing all eight passengers aboard. Amelia, nevertheless, regularly took TAT flights without a thought and added talks promoting the new line to her crowded calendar.

Her main goal, however, was to set more of her own flying records. Amelia had won fame as a passenger on the *Friendship*, but she had contributed little to that flight, and she wanted to start earning the publicity she was getting. To sharpen her piloting skills, she took lessons in February, and in March, after passing a rigorous test, she

The very day she took possession of the plane, she put her name in as a contestant in the first women's cross-country air race, an arduous seven-day sprint over twenty-eight-hundred miles of deserts, mountains, and plains, with a winner's purse of nearly $10,000. On August 18, Amelia and eighteen other flyers set off on the race from Santa Monica, making eighteen stops as they dashed around the country to the finish line in Cleveland, Ohio. From the beginning, the event—dubbed the Powder Puff Derby—was marked by disasters. Flying two thousand feet over Texas, Blanche

became the fourth woman to receive a commercial transport license, the highest rating pilots could receive. She was regularly flying to appearances in her little Avian, but she needed a bigger, better plane to prove her mettle as a flyer. With the money she was making from *Cosmopolitan*, lectures, and the airline, Amelia bought herself a Lockheed Vega. It was the fastest, most powerful heavy monoplane on the market, but Elinor Smith was no fan of the Vega; she called it unstable, with "all the glide potential of a boulder falling off a mountain." Still, the Lockheed was able to fly far and fast, and Amelia loved it.

Noyes saw her plane was on fire, burned her hands after making an emergency landing, and smashed her fuselage as she was taking off again in thick mesquite brush. In Ohio, Ruth Nichols barrelled into a tractor as she was taking off and amazingly, after flipping three times in her airplane, managed to climb out uninjured. In a tragic incident, Marvel Crosson plunged to her death over Arizona when her airplane went into a tailspin and her parachute failed to open after she'd jumped out. Amelia, too, suffered a number of mishaps—a short-circuit in Santa Monica and a smashed propeller in Yuma, Arizona—and she almost had a disastrous finish

To prove her skills as a flyer, Amelia entered the Women's National Air Derby, a dangerous cross-country race, in 1929. Other racers in the derby included (from left) Jessie "Chubbie" Miller; test pilot Claire Fahy; Marvel Crosson, who fell to her death after her plane went into a tailspin over Arizona; Ruth Nichols, who flew into a tractor; actress and flyer Ruth Elder; and wing-walking daredevil Phoebe Omlie.

when she came in for a landing in Cleveland. Elinor Smith watched her bounce the powerful Vega all over the airport, struggling to control the fast plane and frantically braking it to a stop before she cracked it up. Amelia's amateurish flying exposed her lack of air time in the heavy Vega, as well as her raw nerve and "gut courage" in entering the grueling competition. After "one look at her drawn countenance when she flipped up the cockpit hood," Elinor was "filled with admiration" for Amelia and her sheer daring as a flyer and competitor.

Even with the fastest heavy monoplane, Amelia finished third, two hours behind the first-place winner, Louise Thaden. She hadn't won the race as she had hoped, and it was a disaster from G. P.'s point of view, but she was now part of a network of women flyers and able to get one of her long-term organizational plans off the ground.

Two years earlier, she had written to Ruth Nichols with the idea of starting an association of women pilots, and in Cleveland, after the derby, she held a get-together in her hotel suite to talk about launching one. A few months later, in early November, twenty-six women flyers convened on Long Island for a more formal meeting inside a noisy hangar at Curtiss Field. Amelia, whom they liked and respected, said little during the discussion but suggested that they name the group after the number of charter members. The new flying organization soon became known as the Ninety-Nines.

Amelia was making professional strides, but her personal life at that point was approaching a crisis. Dorothy, sick of the rumors and public humiliation, had abruptly walked out on her marriage in the middle of a party G. P. was hosting at Rocknoll. A guest was surprised to see movers

loading her boxes and belongings onto a truck as she followed them out, dressed in traveling clothes. "Didn't you know?" she remarked. "I'm divorcing George." He didn't need her anymore, she casually explained, and she was planning to move to Reno, Nevada, for a quick settlement.

Left Soon after the derby, Amelia (fourth from right) helped launch an association of women pilots called the Ninety-Nines.

G. P. considered Elinor Smith—who daringly flew under four New York City bridges at age seventeen—a potential threat to Amelia's career.

Dorothy's exit meant that Amelia would have to make crucial decisions. If she had ever been in love with G. P., her passion for him, by this time, had apparently cooled. Their lives were closely entwined, however, and she had to carefully consider how she wanted to move forward. In a rare moment of candor, she took Elinor Smith out to lunch and asked her, bluntly, how she thought New York newspapers would react if she married G. P. It didn't seem to be "the romance of the century," Elinor recalled, and marriage seemed an odd prospect for Amelia, who always denied she had any interest in matrimony. Elinor reckoned it would be a marriage of convenience; "given G. P.'s extremely possessive nature," she guessed, it would mean to him that "his prize could never get away." As for Amelia, G. P. "*was* making a lot of money for her," Elinor knew, and if she didn't marry him and G. P. withdrew his help, she could be in a fix.

Elinor knew personally how dangerous it could be to stand in his way. Months earlier, he had vowed to destroy her career as a flyer, since he thought that, potentially, she could be a threat to Amelia. Elinor also believed that G. P. had used shameless tactics to book Amelia's appearances after the *Friendship* flight, pressuring lecture bureaus to substitute his "Lady Lindy" in bookings that had originally been scheduled around the country for Lady Heath. She was sure that Amelia knew nothing about G. P.'s schemes, but she revealed all his business manipulations to her during the lunch. Amelia seemed surprised and embarrassed. "He'll do anything he thinks will protect my interests," she tried to explain; "I just don't know how else to apologize for him." Still, Amelia was open to the possibility of marriage. She knew what she wanted, Elinor sensed, and where she wanted to go.

Amelia may have seemed almost ready to take the plunge, but G. P. was apparently beginning to get cold feet about ending his marriage. Every day, behind Amelia's back, he was writing sad, miserable letters to Dorothy in Reno, pleading with her to change her mind and come back to Rye. Dorothy, however, had made her decision, and on the morning of December 19, 1929, she got her divorce. She was free and unfettered—but for Amelia and G. P., the pressures were mounting. Reporters instantly telephoned Amelia, asking if she was going to become the next Mrs. Putnam, and in the glare of publicity, she abruptly backed off, denying categorically that any wedding was in the works. Weeks later, when Dorothy unexpectedly married Frank Upton, reporters again started circling Amelia. "I am not engaged to anyone," she responded time after time. "Mr. Putnam is my publisher," she insisted—"that's all." Suddenly gun-shy about getting tied down, Amelia was now "unsold on marriage," she explained to a friend, and couldn't help seeing it as a kind of a cage.

What she wanted now, above all, was the freedom to continue living life on her own terms. She was still in New York—having moved with Amy to the American Women's Association club building near *Cosmopolitan*—and she had a live-in secretary to help her stay on top of her mountains of correspondence and a schedule so tight she barely had time, she said, to wash her hair. She was still writing articles, and she was flying, too, setting a new women's speed record that summer in her Lockheed Vega. Her association with TAT, however, had come to an end. The company was having crippling financial problems, and Amelia began working instead with a new start-up service, the New York–Philadelphia–Washington Airway Corporation. The line had been founded by two of her colleagues—Paul Collins, a former airmail flyer and TAT's general superintendant, and Eugene Vidal, a handsome, brawny former college football star and Olympic decathlete who had served in the army air corps and taught aeronautics at West Point before joining TAT's technical staff. Both men had been fired from TAT in the financial shake-up, but they had come up with an idea for a new airline that would fly short, heavily trafficked routes, every hour on the hour, with reasonable fares.

Gene had first met Amelia on a plane when they were working for TAT, and he was struck by her modesty, equanimity, and quiet confidence. He thought she'd be an asset in the new airline he was already planning, and he and Paul soon asked her to join them as vice president of public relations. Financed by Philadelphia backers Nicholas and Charles Townsend Ludington, the new enterprise, known as "the Ludington Line," started flying between New York, Washington, and Philadelphia on September 1, and the service got off to a strong start. In its first ten days of operation, it had a record 1,557 customers and, Amelia proudly reported, nearly half of those paying passengers were women.

She was "staggered" with work, flying parts of the Ludington Line at least every other day, but in the middle of the month she had to make a sudden,

In 1930, Amelia signed on as vice president of a new air service, the Ludington Line, started by two of her TAT colleagues, Eugene Luther Vidal, left, and Paul Collins.

unscheduled trip back to Los Angeles. Edwin, who had remarried, was now gravely ill with stomach cancer, and he wanted to see her. Amelia stayed with her father for four days, settling all his affairs—even writing his obituary—before heading back to New York on September 23. Edwin died eight hours after she left his side, and his death was a blow. Two days later, upset and unsteady, Amelia piloted her Vega to Norfolk, Virginia, where she was scheduled to deliver a lecture. As she was landing at Hampton Roads Naval Air Station, she cracked up her plane—due to a "mechanical failure," she explained—and badly gashed her scalp.

She kept her engagement, her head turbaned with bandages, but she wasn't herself. Amelia was in pain, physically and emotionally not "up to snuff," and her Vega was so badly smashed it had to be entirely rebuilt.

G. P., too, was now at a crossroads. In August 1930, eight months after his divorce, he was out of a job, having sold his stake in his publishing company to a thirty-year-old cousin.

He had "no definite plans for the future," though he soon joined another publishing firm, Brewer & Warren, as a vice president and published a biography that he'd written of a polar explorer. He dedicated his book, *Andrée: The Record of a Tragic Adventure,* to "a favorite aeronaut about to embark on new adventures," and Amelia was a continuing, perhaps increasing, preoccupation. He wanted to marry her, despite her reluctance, and he proposed to her on as many as six occasions. Her answer had always been a definite "no"—but G. P. popped the question again that autumn inside a hangar where Amelia was warming up her plane, and this time she finally agreed, simply nodding her head and patting his arm as she clambered into the cockpit for takeoff.

They made no announcement, but the engagement made headlines when reporters learned that they had taken out a marriage license. Amelia wanted a private wedding, with no word to reporters, and she traveled to Connecticut on Sunday, November 8, to sign the document and perhaps even marry G. P. in a quiet ceremony at his mother's home. Any plans for a wedding, however, were abruptly shelved when Amelia discovered that G. P. had alerted the press, and she left in a rage the next morning for New York and Washington. When reporters called her about the story, she claimed she knew nothing at all about a marriage

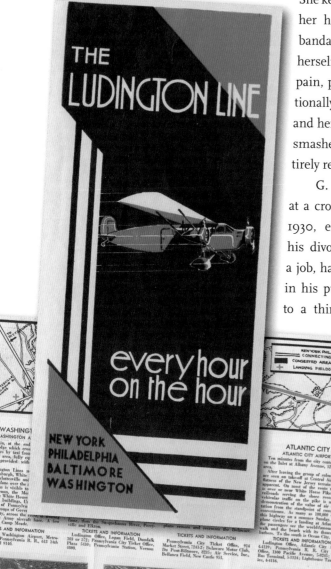

license, stating only that she might get married "some time in the next fifty years." G. P., for his part, confirmed that they had taken out a license, although the wedding date, he acknowledged, was "still indefinite."

Amelia's ambivalence about marriage had agonizingly resurfaced. A year earlier, she had asked Elinor Smith how the New York press would react if she married G. P. Now, she wanted to find out for herself before she made a decision. At the end of December she invited two top aviation reporters—Lauren P. "Deke" Lyman of the *New York Times* and Carl Allen of the *World Telegram*—to her apartment, where she asked them, to their astonishment, if they thought that she should marry G. P. It was a profoundly embarrassing question for the reporters, who had never discussed any personal matters with Amelia and were aware, and wary, of G. P.'s power and influence in publishing circles. Allen finally replied, "It seems to me, Amelia, that the question you have just asked Mr. Lyman and me really contains its own answer; either you should be able to make up your own mind or you should put off getting married until you yourself can decide." It could be, he noted, "that you need him as much or more than he needs you—and one of the supposedly solider cornerstones of marriage is mutual need and mutual respect." Amelia shook hands with them firmly as they left, saying that the conversation had been helpful.

Within weeks, she had made her decision. Married life with G. P., she realized, would not be easy. Ten years older than she was and set in his ways, he could be exasperating—irascible and moody, with an ungenerous streak—while Amelia was quiet and calm and shunned confrontation. But she had always been attracted to risk—and besides, G. P. would handle all the "grubby" details of her public career and make sure she earned enough money

to fund her passion for flying. Amelia also knew that he respected her need for autonomy and independence—he was "the one person," she judged, "who could put up with me"—and theirs could be an amiable, even affectionate partnership.

On a cold clear Saturday in February 1931, Amelia married G. P. at his mother's home overlooking Long Island Sound. A family friend, Judge Anderson, performed the casual ceremony, witnessed only by G. P.'s mother and uncle and the

Above In February 1931, Amelia married G. P. at his mother's home in Noank, Connecticut.

Opposite A brochure for the Ludington Line, an hourly shuttle service to cities on the East Coast

judge's son. In front of a crackling fire, G. P. and Amelia—who was "quite delicate looking" in a brown suit, a light brown blouse, and brown shoes and stockings—repeated their

Dear Gyp,

There are some things which should be writ before we are married—things we have talked over before most of them.

You must know again my reluctance to marry, my feeling that I shatter thereby chances in work which means most to me. I feel the move just now as foolish as anything I could ever do. I know there may be compensations but have no heart to look ahead.

On our life together, I want you to understand I shall not hold you to any medieval code of faithfulness to me nor shall I consider myself so bound to you. If we can be honest about affections for others which may come to either of us the difficulties of such situations may be avoided.

Please let us not interfere with the other's work or play. Nor let the world see our private joys or disagreements. In this connection I may have to keep some place apart—where I may retreat from even an attractive cage, to be myself.

I must exact a cruel promise and that is you will let me go in a year if we find no happiness together. (And this for me too.)

I will try to do my best in every way and give you fully of that part of me you know and seem to want.

A

February 7, 1931

vows, and G. P. slipped a platinum ring, borrowed from his mother, onto her finger.

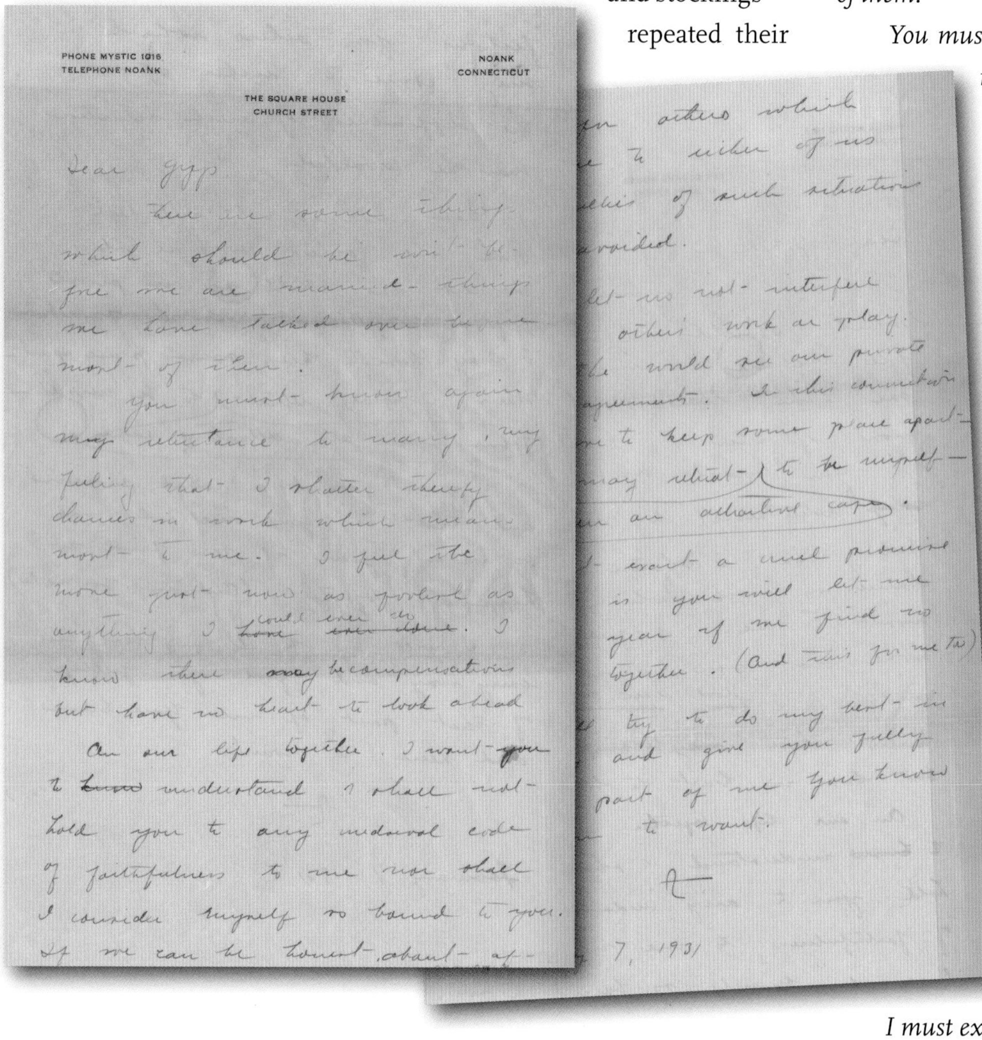

He must have been reeling. Shortly before the ceremony, she had handed him a note, written in pencil on his mother's stationery, with a serious, steady look on her face that conveyed its importance. The letter, written that morning, unequivocably stated her terms for keeping the "cage door" open after the wedding:

G. P., stunned by the letter's "brutal" frankness, simply smiled and nodded, taking Amelia's

hand, and the wedding proceeded without further displays of affection. Afterward, after sipping a glass of wine, Amelia slipped on her brown fur coat; G. P. telephoned his secretary to announce the marriage, and the newlyweds drove off, pledging to be back at their desks again on Monday morning.

Amelia hadn't told Amy and Muriel that she was planning to marry; they both opposed the match because G. P. was a decade older and a divorced man. After the wedding, however, Amelia wired the news to Muriel—"Over the broomstick with GP today stop break news gently to mother"—and by the end of the month, she was writing

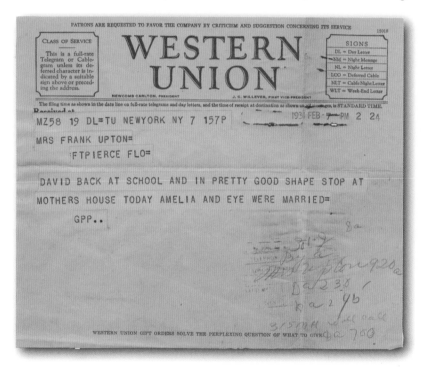

G. P. sent his ex-wife Dorothy, who was already remarried, this telegram announcing his marriage to Amelia.

directly and reassuringly to Amy about her marriage. "I am much happier than I expected I could ever be in that state," Amelia confided. "I believe the whole thing was for the best. Of course," she added, "I go on the same way as before as far as business is concerned. I haven't changed at all and will only be busier I suppose."

Days later, as she settled into Rocknoll, Amelia asked Amy to send her old family quilts, candlesticks, music books, and "things which were Grandma's." She was enjoying the pleasures of domestic life, especially the quiet comforts of the home in Rye. She and G. P. often spent weeknights in a small Manhattan apartment, but Rocknoll, for Amelia, was a soothing sanctuary. She unwound in its cozy, eclectic rooms lined with books and exotic mementos from around the world, and she loved getting her hands dirty in the garden—digging, uncovering crocuses, and nibbling the sweet little yellow tomatoes that she liked to grow. She was also a doting stepmother to G. P.'s sons, canceling all her outside engagements and getting G. P. to do the same whenever the boys came to Rye. Eighteen-year-old David visited more often than nine-year-old Junie, who had contracted polio, but whenever either of them came to stay, she loved taking them picnicking, horseback riding, and sailing and swimming out on Long Island Sound. David, who had been on expeditions to the Arctic and the Galapagos Islands, appreciated his stepmother's daring, curiosity, and attractive looks. She was graceful and long-legged, he observed, with "a lovely head, like a beautiful choirboy's," and wore elegant clothes—though she was so skinny, he recalled, that "she looked like a bag of bones in a bathing suit."

Amelia and G. P., David believed, were deeply connected, but they were also independent within marriage, with a "system of dual control." Amelia kept her own name, and they maintained separate finances, splitting their expenses exactly in half. "Ours is a reasonable and contented partnership," Amelia noted, "my husband with his solo jobs, and I with mine." Still, the two of them worked and played "a great deal together," and their calendars were filled with countless commitments.

There was constant pressure, however, to keep Amelia's name, and her flying career, in the news. In December, she had been invited to pilot in the headlines. In April, she set a new women's altitude record in the "windmill of the air," climbing 18,415 feet, and in May—after being "almost

an experimental type of aircraft—half airplane and half helicopter, as G. P. later described it. Called an autogiro, it could land "like a turkey buzzard," without rolling to a stop, and it took off in less space and climbed more steeply than conventional airplanes. The autogiro was the latest development in aviation and seemed a perfect chance for Amelia to get back inarticulate," with her knees "a bit wobbly," from a tonsillectomy—she and a mechanic took off on a coast-to-coast flight in the novel aircraft, a commercial tour for the Beech-Nut Packing Company. Amelia was essentially piloting a flying billboard, Beech-Nut emblazoned on its side, as she attempted to make the first cross-country autogiro flight.

The comfortable house in Rye was a sanctuary where Amelia loved to relax in book-filled rooms and dig in the garden.

In 1931, she set off on a cross-country tour, sponsored by Beech-Nut, in a new kind of aircraft—an autogiro—that looked like a "flying wind-mill" and crashed a number of times, though she wasn't hurt.

By the time she reached Oakland eight days later, however, another autogiro pilot had unexpectedly beaten her to the transcontinental record. So Amelia took off again, this time for the East Coast, on the first round-trip cross-country flight in the "flying windmill." It was a slow journey. In twenty-one days, Amelia made a total of seventy-six stops. Flying an autogiro was barely faster than traveling by car, since it cruised at about eighty miles an hour—slower in headwinds—and had to stop for refueling about every 150 miles. It was also hard to control, and there were unfortunate mishaps. Amelia was demonstrating the craft at an air show in Abilene, Texas, when it unexpectedly began losing altitude. She brought it down quickly, away from the crowd, but she hit some parked cars and damaged the giro so badly that she cancelled her tour and travelled back to the East Coast by train. In a bruising rebuke, the Department of Commerce officially reprimanded her for carelessness and poor judgment in the crack-up. After crashing again, when her autogiro came down on a fence in Camden, New Jersey, Amelia had had it with giros, swearing that she would "never get in one of these machines again."

But the fact was, she needed the work, so she agreed to take off on another autogiro tour in the middle of August. A month later, she was demonstrating the aircraft at the Michigan State Fair when it suddenly dropped twenty feet and slammed to the ground. G. P., who was in the crowd, saw the crash and raced over to Amelia and the smoking wreck, but he caught his legs in a guy wire as he was running and flew into the air, landing on his back, spraining his ankle, and breaking three ribs.

Amelia wasn't injured, but she was, she felt, "jumping through hoops" like a "little white horse in the circus." The giro tours seemed like a sideshow, and she wanted to tackle something bigger, more challenging, and more important. She was assuming new leadership roles in aviation; in April she had been voted vice president of the National Aeronautic Association, its very first woman officer, and in September she was elected president of the Ninety-Nines. That fall, she and G. P. decided that the timing was right for her to start writing a second book, which she titled *The Fun of It*, and Amelia spent most of that winter drafting the manuscript.

She was also quietly hatching another plan. One morning in early 1932, she was sitting at the breakfast table with G. P. when she suddenly lowered her morning paper and asked him slowly, "Would you mind if I flew the Atlantic?" He felt, he recalled, "something akin to elation" as well as "a clutch at the heart." Crossing the Atlantic by airplane was still a very dangerous business, and no one had been able to repeat Lindbergh's solo achievement. After the *Friendship* flight, some twenty planes with crews had also made it safely to the other side, but two pilots had perished making solo attempts, and Lady Heath, a seasoned long-distance flyer, believed that it would be "plain

suicide" and "madness" for any woman to try to fly across the Atlantic Ocean alone.

Wearing a flight suit, Amelia set an 18,415-foot women's altitude record in the autogiro.

Even so, several crack women pilots were determined to follow "the Lindbergh Trail" over the Atlantic, including Elinor Smith, Ruth Nichols, and a fearless acrobatic flyer named Laura Ingalls. Amelia had been dreaming about making the attempt ever since her first crossing in the *Friendship*, as "a self-justification," she explained—proving to herself, and everyone else, that she and other women with adequate experience would be able to do it. Now, with around a thousand more flying hours under her belt, she felt ready to try.

Her Vega, rebuilt since she wrecked it in Norfolk, was an ideal plane for long-distance flying, and Amelia believed that by careful preparation, she'd be able to reduce the risks.

For assistance, she and G. P. turned to Bernt Balchen, an exceptional pilot and technician who had made pioneering Atlantic and Antarctic flights with Commander Richard Byrd. On a Sunday in early April, they invited Bernt over for lunch and let him in on their plans. "Am I ready to do it? Is the ship ready?" Amelia asked him. "Will you help me?" "Yes," he replied, agreeing to assist her and keep the plan secret to avoid the stress of publicity. For the next month, while Bernt focused on refitting and readying the plane, Amelia was able to live a normal life, "fit, happy and rested, physically and mentally." Friends came to Rocknoll, as always, for meals or overnight stays; Amelia dug in the garden, took care of her Ninety-Nines business, proofed the galleys of her book, and raked leaves in the yard with G. P. The two of them seemed to be a close team, and there was a sense of order and calm in the flow of their days.

There was just one major hurdle ahead—she had to learn how to fly blind, using instruments alone, so she'd be able to keep her course during perilous storms over the Atlantic. While she practiced her flying, Bernt and mechanic Eddie Gorski worked on the crimson and gold Vega at Teterboro Airport in New Jersey—strengthening its fuselage and installing new instruments, including a drift indicator, a gyroscope, and periodic and magnetic compasses. They also installed extra fuel tanks in the cabin and wings—boosting the fuel capacity to 420 gallons and giving the plane a cruising radius of some 3,200 miles—as a well as a new supercharged

Opposite Dressed in feminine clothes, at the controls

This page In 1932, Amelia set out to be the first woman to fly solo across the Atlantic. With the expert help of technical adviser Bernt Balchen (left), she refitted her Lockheed Vega (rendered below) for the dangerous flight.

500-horsepower Wasp engine. Another accomplished pilot, Major Edwin Aldrin—father of the future moonwalking astronaut—supervised the fueling of the plane and specified its gas and oil. From the start, Amelia had told Bernt that she would quit, no harm done, if he ever thought that she or her Vega wouldn't be able to make it. But Bernt never

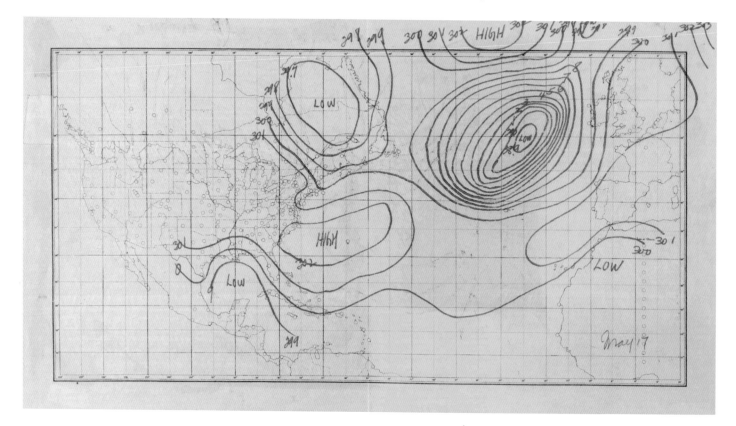

wavered, and his unflagging confidence was crucial in sustaining her own courage.

G. P., meanwhile, was at work on publicity plans. He was hoping she would solo across the Atlantic on May 20, the fifth anniversary of Lindbergh's flight. Her route would be different from Lindbergh's, however, and considerably shorter. Although she would try to reach Paris, where Lindbergh had landed, she would take off from Harbor Grace, Newfoundland, instead of New York, and make her first landfall in the British Isles. Amelia would need to leave for Newfoundland, at the latest, by May 19 in order to make her dash across the Atlantic on "Lindbergh Day," but conditions weren't looking at all promising. Every day, ready to start, she made the thirty-mile drive out to Terterboro, but with bad weather ahead, she had to turn around and head back to Rye. Her nerves weren't fraying, however, and she wasn't thinking too much about dangers. "I always feel you have to take some chances on long-distance flights," she explained to Ruth Nichols, "so I don't bother to go into all the possible accidents that might happen." Amelia simply didn't think about crack-ups; in her mind, according to Ruth, "you would go when your number was up and not before," and meantime, she added, "there was no use worrying about it."

Finally, on the morning of May 19, Amelia arrived at Teterboro and learned that the weather was looking clear all the way. She raced back to Rye, threw on her jodhpurs, a silk shirt, and a leather jacket, grabbed her comb and a toothbrush, her

wishers from the Vega, she gave it the gun and took off in a southwest wind, heading out over the ocean.

Amelia flew through clear skies for about three hours. Then suddenly her altimeter failed, and she had no idea from that point on how high or low she was flying over the darkening ocean. Then flames started shooting out of her exhaust, and a raging electrical storm tossed her around violently for about an hour. Soon after, ice started coating her wings, adding dangerous weight, so she flew lower to warmer air until she could see waves breaking beneath her. When a low fog rolled in, Amelia had to climb higher for safety, groping for a level where she'd avoid icing her wings or ditching her plane in the Atlantic. Gasoline was dripping down her neck and shoulder from a leaky tank, her exhaust manifold was vibrating dangerously, she was flying blind, and she wasn't sure how long her fuel supply would be able to hold out. So at dawn, after ten hours of harrowing flying, Amelia spotted a tanker off the Irish coast and thought she'd better start looking for a place to land.

A few hours later, over the Irish countryside, she started following a railroad, thinking it might lead to an airport. But Amelia saw only miles of green pastures and farms everywhere around and finally decided to

flying suit, a couple of scarves, a thermos bottle for soup, and a few cans of tomato juice, and dashed back to the airport. Twenty minutes later, she was in the air, heading up to Newfoundland in the Vega with Bernt and Eddie. Amelia napped in the back while Bernt handled the plane, and they stopped overnight in St. John before reaching Harbor Grace the next afternoon. Amelia had always been able to drift off to sleep as soon as she shut her eyes, and she napped on the flight from St. John, and again in Harbor Grace, so she'd be rested and fresh for her long night of Atlantic flying.

At six o'clock that evening, May 20, 1932, Bernt gave Amelia the all-clear. Everything was ready, and she listened—as "quiet and unobtrusive as a young Lindbergh," he remembered— as he went over the route and the weather; she showed "no signs of anxiety or fear," a reporter said. Amelia shook hands with Bernt and Eddie, then crawled into the cockpit of her big plane and started the engine, nodding her head as they pulled out the chocks. At 7:12, waving at her well-

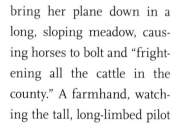

bring her plane down in a long, sloping meadow, causing horses to bolt and "frightening all the cattle in the county." A farmhand, watching the tall, long-limbed pilot climb out of the plane, couldn't tell if it was a man or a woman. "Have you flown far?" he asked Amelia. "From America," she said matter-of-factly; stunned, he fetched her a glass of water and invited her into his cottage to wash the grease from her face. Soon after, Amelia hitched a ride into Londonderry, five miles away, to telephone G. P. and give him the great news. She had done it. She had flown across the Atlantic again, this time alone—a feat that no one, man or woman, had been able to accomplish except Lindbergh.

By time she returned to her plane, word was out, and excited crowds and reporters were starting to swarm. The next day, after spending a quiet night in a nearby home, she good-naturedly agreed to taxi her Vega around the pasture, reenacting her landing for the benefit of the newsreel cameras. That afternoon, she took off in a Paramount News plane for Croydon airport, near London, where she graciously posed for more news photos in the pouring rain. Though Amelia had meticulously planned her flight, she hadn't given any thought to what she'd do after her arrival, so U.S. Ambassador Andrew Mellon whisked her away to the American Embassy in London. Once again, she was deluged with congratulatory cables—many more of them, this time, from international celebrities and heads of state, including President Herbert Hoover, Britain's King George V, the king of Belgium, and Crown Prince Wilhelm of Germany. A painfully touching tribute arrived from Charles Lindbergh and his wife, Anne, who had

only learned ten days before that their one-year-old baby, Charles Jr., had been murdered by kidnappers.

There was no time to recover and rest; Amelia was again in the world's spotlight, stranded in London with only the clothes on her back. So the next morning, wearing an outfit she borrowed from the ambassador's daughter, she went shopping at Selfridge's, which was planning to exhibit her Vega in its store windows. The next eleven days were a brilliant blur of formal honors, public appearances, and receptions. Amelia broadcast a radio address to the American people; visited the Prince of Wales in his private rooms, where they "talked shop" about flying, and danced with him at a charity ball; stayed with Lady Astor, the only woman member of Parliament; met George Bernard Shaw; wrote a postcript for her book on her Atlantic solo; and made so many speeches that she eventually had to speak in a whisper and take to her bed with a sore throat.

It was too much to handle, and she wanted G. P. by her side. On May 27, he left New York on the *Olympic* and sailed to Cherbourg, France, where he met Amelia on a yacht that had carried her across the English Channel. Together, they boarded a train for Paris, Lindbergh's historic destination. The crowds that met her were so frenzied they surged onto the tracks at the Gare St.-Lazare, forcing the train to stop, and jammed the streets, cheering, as Amelia and G. P. motored to their hotel. All of Paris was crazy for "the girl Lindbergh." The French government awarded her the Cross of the Legion of Honor, which it had bestowed on Lindbergh five years earlier; she was royally wined and dined by the international set; and she was greeted and gifted with so many flowers that G. P. was "red-eyed and weeping" with hay fever. On June 8, the couple headed to Rome, where Amelia was welcomed by Italy's air

Page 106 Amelia on the wing of her Vega after landing in Ireland; congratulatory cables, including a telegram from the Lindberghs, who had recently learned of the murder of their kidnapped baby

Page 107 Landing in London, Amelia was again the center of international attention.

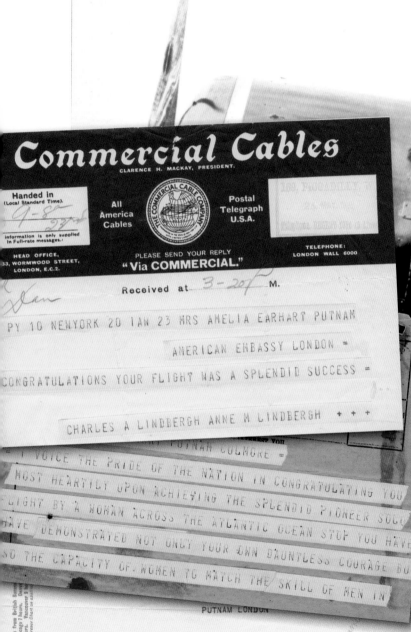

Commercial Cables

CLARENCE H. MACKAY, PRESIDENT.

Handed in
(Local Standard Time).

All
America
Cables

Postal
Telegraph
U.S.A.

Information is only supplied
in Full-rate messages.

HEAD OFFICE,
33, WORMWOOD STREET,
LONDON, E.C.2.

PLEASE SEND YOUR REPLY
"Via COMMERCIAL."

TELEPHONE:
LONDON WALL 6000

Received at 3-20 M.

PY 10 NEWYORK 20 IAN 23 MRS AMELIA EARHART PUTNAM

AMERICAN EMBASSY LONDON =

CONGRATULATIONS YOUR FLIGHT WAS A SPLENDID SUCCESS =

CHARLES A LINDBERGH ANNE M LINDBERGH + + +

PUTNAM COLACRE =

I VOICE THE PRIDE OF THE NATION IN CONGRATULATING YOU
MOST HEARTILY UPON ACHIEVING THE SPLENDID PIONEER SOLO
FLIGHT BY A WOMAN ACROSS THE ATLANTIC OCEAN STOP YOU HAVE
HAVE DEMONSTRATED NOT ONLY YOUR OWN DAUNTLESS COURAGE BUT
SO THE CAPACITY OF WOMEN TO MATCH THE SKILL OF MEN IN

PUTNAM LONDON

WE KNEW YOU COULD DO IT AND NOW YOU HAVE STOP
CHEERS CONGRATULATIONS MUCH LOVE

MOTHER AND MURIEL

minister and the entire staff of the air force and congratulated by the crown prince and Premier Mussolini. Five days later, they were charmingly entertained in Brussels by Belgium's king and queen, who awarded her the Cross of the Chevalier of the Order of Leopold and took her snapshot, Amelia recalled, with an "ancient little camera."

Finally, spent, sated, and celebrated beyond all expectation, they boarded the *Île de France* on June 15 and headed back to New York City. Amelia was sailing the same ocean she had flown over just a few weeks before, and she had time now to savor the magnitude of her achievement. She was the

Above Amelia leaves the American embassy, where she was staying, for rounds of appearances in the British capital.

Far right Traveling to Paris, she was welcomed and celebrated as "the girl Lindbergh."

Right A medal commemorating her record flight

first woman and only the second person to solo across the Atlantic Ocean. She was the only person in the world who had flown over that ocean twice. She had set the speed record for an Atlantic crossing and a nonstop distance record for women flyers. But her greatest satisfaction came from the sheer thrill of adventure and deep pleasure of proving that she was up to the task. She was now "a kind of public Joan of Arc," a hero and legend—but most important to Amelia, she was a first-class flyer, and she was at the controls.

Amelia, with G. P.
in Paris, waving to
crowds gathered out-
side their hotel

5
HIGH FLYER

A melia had proven her prowess to the world and to herself, earning her place beside Lindbergh in the pantheon of heroic flyers. Probably never again, a writer predicted, would she be able to walk the streets of any city without being pulled and prodded and "surrounded by the maddening crowd."

Her homecoming in New York City on the morning of June 20 was an astounding tribute. As the *Île de France* dropped anchor in New York Bay, sounding its deep-throated siren, it was echoed by welcoming whistles from vessels waiting in the harbor and the thunder of engines above, as army, navy, and national guard pilots swooped and soared in a dazzling air show unmatched since Lindbergh's return to America. While a municipal band played "The Star-Spangled Banner," Amelia, wearing a brown wool suit and brown linen hat, stepped off the liner onto a boat filled with official greeters, including Bernt Balchen, Gene Vidal, Paul Collins, Ruth Elder, Amy Guest, and even Frank Hawks, who had taken her up in an airplane for the first time twelve years before. She was then raucously welcomed by thousands as she motored down Broadway, dodging blizzards of ticker tape and waving at crowds so excited they rushed through police lines onto the street until reinforcements were able to restore order.

The next day, in Washington, D.C., she reaped historic honors. After a White House reception, she traveled to the Capitol and stood in the well of the Senate as legislators came up to her, one by one, and personally offered their congratulations. Fifteen minutes later, Amelia was cheered by the entire House of

AWARDED BY THE
NATIONAL GEOGRAPHIC SOCIETY
TO
AMELIA EARHART
FIRST WOMAN TO ACHIEVE
A SOLO TRANSATLANTIC FLIGHT
MAY·20·21
1932

Above Special gold medal awarded to Amelia by the National Geographic Society honoring her Atlantic solo

Above Amelia waving to New York crowds in 1932

Right Frank Hawks, who gave Amelia her first ride in an airplane, greeted her when she stepped off the *Île de France* in New York Harbor.

Representatives, whose members rose to their feet as a body when she was introduced. That evening, after she returned to the White House for a formal dinner, President Hoover accompanied her to Constitution Hall, where he bestowed on her the special gold medal of the National Geographic Society, the country's highest honor for geographic achievement. Amelia, its very first woman recipient, accepted the tribute as an audience packed with scientists, military officers, and nearly four thousand senators, congressmen, jurists, and diplomats from twenty-two countries stood and applauded.

Back in New York the following day, Amelia was honored by the Explorers Club as well as fifty civic groups and women's organizations. The appreciation of her record flight, she protested, was completely overwhelming and far "out of proportion," she said, "to the deed itself," but the parades and civic receptions continued nonstop, along with informal tributes—including a new dance, the "Earhart Hop," featuring a whirl resembling a tailspin and "a sudden dip signifying an air pocket." Amelia's latest book, *The Fun of It*, was now on sale, and notices and reviews

72D CONGRESS
1ST SESSION

S. J. RES. 165

IN THE SENATE OF THE UNITED STATES

MAY 9 (calendar day, MAY 24), 1932

Mr. WALCOTT introduced the following joint resolution; which was read twice, considered, and agreed to

JOINT RESOLUTION

Authorizing the President of the United States to present the distinguished-flying cross to Amelia Earhart Putnam.

Resolved by the Senate and House of Representatives of the United States of America in Congress assembled, That the President of the United States is authorized to present the distinguished-flying cross to Amelia Earhart Putnam for displaying heroic courage and skill as a navigator, at the risk of her life, by her nonstop flight in her plane, unnamed, from Harbor Grace, Newfoundland, to Londonderry, Ireland, on May 20, 1932, by which she became the first and only woman, and the second person, to cross the Atlantic Ocean in a plane in solo flight, and also established new records for speed and elapsed time between the two continents.

were keeping her name in the news all over the country.

Despite all the festivities, however, Amelia felt energized and strong. She was, Elinor Smith said, an "iron butterfly," with natural stamina and the ability, she now realized, to stay awake and alert on long overnight hauls. Her grueling flight across the Atlantic, she reported, hadn't been

Across the Atlantic with AMELIA EARHARDT

especially draining; she had danced all night "lots of times," she claimed, "and flying all night isn't very much." Amelia had a thrilling new awareness of her "hidden powers," combined with the excitement she always felt when pushing her own limits and accomplishing "first-time things." She wanted to prove again that she deserved at least a fraction of the praise she was receiving, so she decided, almost immediately after she returned home from Europe, to try setting another difficult long-distance record. This time, she wanted to be the first woman to pilot a plane nonstop across the United States. Her crimson and gold Vega was already outfitted for long-distance flying, but she also wanted to set a speed record, beating the time of 17 hours, 38 minutes that Frank Hawks had achieved on a coast-to-coast flight three years earlier.

Since the winds were more favorable going from west to east, Amelia planned to fly from Los Angeles to Newark, New Jersey. Only eleven days after her homecoming on the *Île de France*, she flew to Los Angeles with G. P. and took off on July 12 on her new cross-country record attempt. A malfunctioning gas line forced her to land in Columbus, Ohio, wrecking her hopes for a nonstop dash, but she did set a women's solo speed record for the 2,559-mile flight. Arriving in New Jersey with an elapsed time of 19 hours, 14 minutes, Amelia characteristically downplayed her disappointment. "I wasn't trying for a record," she said to reporters. The flight, she claimed, "was entirely for practice in navigation."

She returned home to Rocknoll while G. P., now chairman of Paramount's editorial board, stayed on the West Coast. For a couple of weeks, until she flew back to Los Angeles to join him at the Olympic Games, Amelia settled back into her life in Rye, in the company of her cousins Lucy and Kathryn (Katch) Challis. Both of them noted a marked transformation in Amelia. She was radiant, more beautiful than ever; her star was soaring, and so was her confidence.

She invited other guests out to Rocknoll, including Gene Vidal. She and Gene were far more than business associates; there was a powerful chemistry and connection between them. Gene, according to his son, Gore, was "implausibly handsome," a legendary athlete, and a distinguished pilot. Like Amelia, he was passionate about flying, an enthusiasm that G. P., who was chronically airsick, was unable to share. Gene was married—to Nina Gore, the daughter of blind Tennessee Senator Thomas Gore—but they were growing estranged, and he and Amelia were increasingly in each others' orbits. When Amelia traveled west at the end of the month, Gene and Lucy flew to Los Angeles too, and over the next few days, it dawned on Lucy that Gene and Amelia, in some subtle, unspoken way, belonged to each other. There was nothing overt in their behavior; but it could be Amelia was thinking of Gene when she refused the "medieval code of faithfulness" in marriage.

On July 29, the day before the Tenth Olympiad opened in the Los Angeles Coliseum, it was

Amelia who glamorously medaled in L.A. when Vice President Charles Curtis presented her with the Distinguished Flying Cross, awarded by Congress. The next day, the vice president officially opened the Olympic Games, and Amelia, who loved track events, hobnobbed with sports greats and Hollywood stars and drew cheering capacity crowds of her own at a downtown appearance. Ten days after the Games ended, she was back in the air, more focused than ever on her own record-breaking performance. On August 24, she made another try for a nonstop coast-to-coast solo. This time, she pulled it off, flying 19 hours, 7 minutes without a break between L.A. and Newark. She didn't set a speed record, but she added another "first" to her growing list and set a new women's cross-country distance record. It was a perfect flight, Amelia said, but it was longer than any previous solo she'd ever made, and she showed the

Above Amelia with friends and Gene Vidal, seated in front

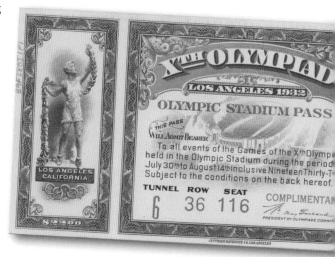

Amelia arrives in Newark, New Jersey, after her record solo flight across the country in 1932.

strain of nearly twenty hours alone in the cockpit. "Don't come near me! If you knew what I feel like—" she snapped as reporters and well-wishers rushed over to greet her, nearly knocking her over. After a few minutes' rest, however, she was able to recover her public face and graceful composure.

That fall, Amelia was back on the road, this time testing her grit in marathon talks and appearances, recounting the story of her Atlantic solo and promoting sales of her new book. Pushing her limits, she often drove all through the night, arriving at hotels early in the morning, stealing a few hours' sleep between bookings, then hitting the road and driving all night again to another town. It was a grind, according to a friend, but Amelia got "her fun the hard way" and threw herself at challenges with no complaint.

In December, she drove out to her father's alma mater, Thiel College, in Greenville, Pennsylvania, where she received an honorary Doctor of Science degree before a packed assembly. It was a "very interesting time," she wrote to Amy. "Everyone remembered Dad as so handsome and bright"; his nickname was "Kid," and his record for scholarship, she discovered, had never been equaled.

Amelia still idolized Edwin, despite all his failings, but she now looked on her mother and sister with a colder eye. Amy had lived with her for a time before she got married, and Amelia and her mother, in those days, had been "as close as ever." As Amelia became more and more famous, however, Amy felt she could only talk to her when she was "holding on to her coat tails." To be sure, however, Amelia was a dutiful daughter. After years of poverty, she was making considerable money, and she generously shared her good fortune with her family. She had paid off her father's $2,000 mortgage before he died, and she sent Amy a regular monthly allowance out of her own earnings. As de facto head of the family, however, Amelia could also be sharply directive and disapproving. Amy was now living with Muriel, who had married businessman Albert Morrissey in 1929. By the end of 1931, the couple had two children, as well as serious marital and financial problems. Amelia had loaned Muriel $2,500 to purchase "a decent house," but she resented the fact that Amy was spending all of her time cleaning and looking after the children. Amelia was also incensed that Amy gave her allowance to Muriel, and she took an increasingly high-handed tone in her correspondence. "I am very much displeased," she wrote to her mother, "at the use you have put what I hoped you would save. I am not working to help Albert, nor Pidge

much as I care for her . . . I do not mean to be harsh," she scolded Amy, "but I know the family failing about money."

Close relations were strained, but Amelia was expanding her circle, winning powerful, high-profile new friends and supporters. In November 1932, New York Governor Franklin Roosevelt and his wife, Eleanor, invited Amelia for an overnight visit at their family home in Hyde Park, New York. Amelia was scheduled to give a lecture in nearby

At the end of that year, her father's alma mater, Thiel College, awarded her an honorary Doctor of Science degree.

Collegium Thielense

Evangelicae Lutheranae Ecclesiae
In Pennsylvaniorum Republica

Omnibus has litteras Prefecturis

✳ SALUTEM ✳

Nos Praeses et Professoris Collegii Thielensis consentientibus honorandis ac reverendis in Comitiis Sollemnibus

Amelia Earhart

honoris causa, ad gradum

DOCTORIS SCIENTIAE

admisimus, eique dedimus et concessimus omnia insignia et iura ad hunc gradum pertinentia.

Cujus in testimonium et nomina nostra et Curatorum Scribae manum et Collegii Sigillum apposuimus. Datus Sedibus Academicis apud Pennsylvanios die undecimo Decembris, Anno Domini MCMXXXII.

Curatorum Praeses
Curatorum Scriba
Praeses

Taken in Utica.

Poughkeepsie, and before the event, she and G. P. joined the couple for an informal dinner. Two weeks earlier, Roosevelt had been elected president of the United States, and Eleanor, an independent, accomplished woman at forty-eight, was worried about the limited, confining role she would have to play as the new first lady. She, like Amelia, was a path-breaking public figure who had built her own business and cared deeply about the welfare of struggling families. She was also, like Amelia, competitive and physically daring; Eleanor's happiest moment, she confided, was making the

first field hockey team when she was at boarding school. The two women recognized each other as kindred spirits, and Eleanor introduced Amelia at her appearance later that night. "I hope to know Miss Earhart more and more," she declared, "but I never hope to admire her more than I do now. She has done," the first-lady-to-be added, "so many things which I have always wanted to do."

One of those things was learning how to fly an airplane, and Amelia quietly offered to give Eleanor piloting lessons. As a first step, she arranged for the necessary physical exam, and on

January 18, Eleanor forwarded Amelia her new student pilot permit. The next step, however, was getting Franklin's consent to the plan. "I will let you know if I am successful with him," Eleanor wrote Amelia—adding in longhand, at the end of the note, "he won't let me now but perhaps later I can persuade him!"

Amelia's own public profile that month was higher than ever. *Vogue* magazine called her "The First Lady of the Sky," and the *New York Times* named her "The Outstanding Aviation Star of 1932." Still, in the throes of the Depression, Amelia was under financial pressure; she did endorsements—for B.G. spark plugs, Stanovo aviation gasoline and oil, Wasp and Hornet engines, and Franklin automobiles—and made frenzied rounds of lectures and appearances around the country. This particular tour, she admitted to Amy, was "much more intensive than I had planned, because the management [G. P.] kept trying to squeeze in more, and in these times I thought I might as well do as much and get as much I could."

Amelia was "a bit fed up" with the constant travel, but she enjoyed, more and more, having a public platform to speak out on issues she cared deeply about. She always liked fighting for principle, and her most absorbing concern, according to G. P., was equal opportunity for women. In countless interviews and lectures as she crossed the country, Amelia argued, with quiet confidence and charm, that qualified women should be considered equally with men for any job and that individual aptitude, not sex, should be the grounds for evaluating a person's ability. She was also "utterly and completely" opposed to war and even proposed drafting women and old people—occasionally drawing shocked gasps from audience members—as a way of putting an end to combat.

Top and bottom Letters to Amelia from Eleanor Roosevelt, who admired her and wanted to learn how to fly

Amelia's personal ambitions, observed pilot Louise Thaden, were always secondary to her "insatiable desire to get women into the air," and

Eleanor Roosevelt, Amelia knew, was a persuasive model. At the end of April, soon after the inauguration, the Roosevelts invited Amelia and G. P. to the White House as overnight guests. Eleanor had just been named honorary chairman of the

of the nation and the first lady of the air—dressed elegantly in long satin gowns, white kid gloves, and velvet and brocade evening coats—boarded the plane accompanied by Eleanor's brother, Hall Roosevelt, G. P., and a half dozen women reporters. Amelia switched off the cabin lights so they

After dinner at the White House, Amelia and First Lady Eleanor Roosevelt boarded a plane for a star-filled night flight over Washington, D.C.

United States Amateur Pilots Association, and to celebrate, Amelia and G. P. arranged to have Eastern Air Transport loan them a big two-motored Condor airplane and crew for the evening. After dinner, Amelia invited Eleanor to go skylarking and experience, for the first time, the beauty of night flying. Eleanor was game, so the first lady

could savor the illuminated capital and the gleam of the stars, and she took the controls for a little while—leading the first lady to comment that "it's amusing to think of a girl in white evening dress and high-heeled shoes flying a plane." Eleanor noted that she "would give a lot to do it myself," but she did get to ride up front with the pilot, "lightly fingering the wheel"—an experience, she said, that was "like being on top of the world." The first lady, flush with excitement, wasn't at all ready to call it a night after they landed. Instead, she invited Amelia to try out her shiny new automobile, and the two of them jumped in and gave it a fast spin around the White House grounds.

Amelia, however, needed to make flying news of her own if she wanted to keep filling auditoriums at $300 a lecture. She had sold her Lockheed Vega, stripped of its motor, to the Franklin Institute Museum for an exhibit, and she had bought another used Vega, a later and faster model, which she'd upgraded with her sturdy old 500-horsepower Wasp engine. After trying out the speedy, refurbished plane in June on a quick trip to the Chicago World's Fair, she decided to put it through its paces in a strenuous cross-country flying derby called the Bendix race. First held in 1931, the Bendix had never been open to women, but in June 1933, just two weeks before the race started, officials suddenly announced that women pilots would be eligible for the competition. Amelia and Ruth Nichols both wanted to enter, though they had no time to get their planes in fighting shape and no chance of winning, since the men had faster planes with engines nearly twice as powerful. The coast-to-coast dash from New York to L.A. was set to start on July 1 at Floyd Bennett Field, and both women were primed for the race. Ruth Nichols, however, quickly ran into plane trouble and had to drop out, and Amelia's new Vega, too, was giving her problems. Her engine was overheating, she almost passed out from carbon monoxide inside the cockpit, and her hatch cover blew off, forcing her to land for repairs in Arizona. Amelia knew that she couldn't win, but she finished the race, earning a special $2,500 prize as the first woman pilot to complete the derby.

It was, Amelia said, the most hazardous cross-country flight she had ever made. Five days later, however, she was back in the air, aiming for another transcontinental speed record. Three hours outside Los Angeles, however, her hatch cover blew off again, and she had to hold it closed for seventy-five miles until she could land for repairs in Amarillo, Texas. After two and a half hours, the hatch secured, Amelia resumed her record attempt but was soon close to unconscious again from leaking gas fumes. Landing in Columbus, Ohio—nauseous and faint, with a bruised arm from clutching the hatch cover—she felt weak in the knees, but she walked around, gulping fresh air, until she was able to continue. When Amelia finally arrived in Newark, after flying through squalls over Pennsylvania, she had beaten her own coast-to-coast time by nearly two hours. She was battered and sore, covered with grease, and feeling sick to her stomach from fumes, but she still had the grit to take the wheel of her own car and drive herself home.

That summer, Amelia, who called herself "a chronic vice president," was also busy getting a new air service off the ground. Eastern Air Transport had acquired the Ludington Line in February, and on August 6, she, Gene, and Paul Collins started a new airline flying between Boston and Bangor, Maine, a subsidiary of the Boston & Maine

The cross-country Bendix Race, which opened to women flyers for the first time in 1933, was the starting event of the National Air Races.

Railroad. G. P., meanwhile, was splitting his time between New York and Hollywood, though he wanted to spend time with Amelia and was hoping she'd join him on a business trip he was planning to Paris. Amelia, however, begged off, saying she didn't look forward to "a stuffy ride over for a week and a stuffy one back." So in September, G. P. sailed for Europe by himself on a month-long trip.

While he was gone, Gene frequently came to stay at the house in Rye. With Amelia's help, he had been angling for a job in the Roosevelt administration as the director of the Commerce Department's new Bureau of Aeronautics. There were dozens of candidates for the job but, thanks to Amelia's friendship with the Roosevelts and his own airline experience, Gene was at the top of the list. On September 20, the president appointed him to the post, and Gene traveled to Rocknoll to celebrate with Amelia that very day.

The next month, she was back on the road for a fall tour, hitting the lecture circuit and promoting her new air service in the press. She flew on the Boston & Maine whenever she could, meeting passengers, selling tickets, and drawing huge crowds at promotional events. And when she wasn't lecturing, flying, and stumping for business in frigid New England weather, Amelia was designing clothes.

She had long been interested in flying apparel for women, since for years she had made do with ill-fitting aviation suits designed for men. Now, she and G. P. decided the time was right to launch a groundbreaking new clothing line called "Amelia Fashions," a collection of stylish, practical clothing for the "active woman." By November 1933, Amelia had created fifty pieces of outdoor, travel, and sports apparel. She not only signed every piece, she also designed them herself—selecting every detail and scrap of fabric and draping the clothes on a

dressmaker's dummy in the living room of her Manhattan apartment while a seamstress stitched the garments together at her old sewing machine. The collection featured wrinkle-free dresses, separates, and outerwear made of unusual, practical materials like parachute silk and fabric used for the wings of airplanes. They had clean, simple lines and wearable colors, with aeronautical details like buttons and clasps that were shaped like screws, valves, and miniature propellers. By early 1934, the clothes were carried in special "Amelia Earhart Shops" in Macy's and department stores all over the country, outfitted with model airplanes and show-cases filled with Amelia's own flying clothes and aviation accessories.

She was marketing her line with the same drive and intensity she devoted to all her flights and her public career. According to a Macy's executive, she "was a terrifically honest person," although he thought she was remarkably shy. For someone "who had stood before millions and received their acclaim," he recalled, "she was amazingly diffident in lesser situations. When she came into the store, if there were so much as ten or twelve people in the room, she would seem to shrink into herself." Amelia told the press she was having a "swell time" in the fashion business, but it was "was one of the hardest strains she ever went through," Amy noted, "because she was doing so much at that time." Amelia's work schedule was

Top A sewn-in clothing label and swatches of fabric that Amelia personally chose for her clothing line, "Amelia Fashions"

Opposite The designer modeling one of her dresses in 1934

so draining that she had to drink cream and eat waffles soaking in butter just to keep up her strength and her weight. It proved too much to handle. She couldn't keep up the pace, and she shut down Amelia Fashions by the end of the year.

After her frenetic schedule all winter and spring, she and G. P. finally managed to get away in July for a much-needed vacation. They headed to Wyoming's rugged Absaroka Mountains near Yellowstone Park, where they stayed for a couple of weeks at the Double Dee dude ranch, owned by an old friend of G. P.'s named Carl Dunrud. There, Amelia wrote, in the "crisp peacefulness of the Wyoming mountains," she was finally able to fully relax; it was, she added, a whole world of its own, "refreshing, restful, and remote." Isolated from the pressures of business and fame, she and G. P. spent long, happy days riding pack horses, fly-fishing, and cooking on campfires under the stars. Amelia, Carl Dunrud remembered, "was just one

Amelia gets a haircut on a dude ranch vacation in 1934 and goes fishing with G. P.

of the gang in camp"; it was a welcome relief, for a while, from the stresses of public life and adoring crowds. Wyoming was such a reviving refuge that she and G. P. planned to build a cabin on land they fell in love with "a million miles from fame," noted a friend—a remote property safe from reporters that was a nine-mile trip by packhorse from the nearest road.

In August, rejuvenated and ready to get back to work, Amelia plunged once again into promotional tasks for the Boston & Maine. Her upcoming lecture bookings, however, were looking a little thin. It had been two years since her famed transatlantic solo, and her marketability with audiences was starting to slip. By this time, however, Amelia knew the routine: "I make a record," she explained frankly, "and then I lecture on it. That's where the money comes from. Until it's time to make another record," she added—and now, it seemed, was one of those times.

Amelia had conquered the Atlantic, and "one ocean," she wrote, "naturally led to another." There was still the Pacific to cross. A few pilots had flown it before, but none of them solo, and many had lost their lives on the dangerous open stretch of water between the West Coast and the Hawaiian Islands. One evening in September, Amelia, wearing gold crepe pajamas, looked up suddenly from her reading and told G. P. nonchalantly that she wanted to fly the Pacific—from Hawaii to California, she said, because "it's easier to hit a continent than an island." It was a risky proposal, and as G. P. knew well, it would be an expensive operation to pull together. He set to work right away trying to raise the funds and was quickly able to land a sponsor for the flight, the Hawaiian Sugar Planters Association.

To prepare for her Pacific solo, Amelia moved to Los Angeles, where Lockheed was getting her Vega into flying shape. This time, her technical adviser was Paul Mantz, the president of the Motion Picture Pilots' Association—a stunt flyer and precision pilot who was well versed in the latest aviation technology. Under Paul's supervision, Lockheed boosted the Vega's fuel capacity to 470 gallons and installed new instruments including periodic and magnetic compasses, a tachometer, a directional bank and turn indicator, and two altimeters. Meanwhile, Amelia scrutinized maps with navigation experts

In 1934, she hired Hollwood stunt pilot Paul Mantz as her technical adviser to help her prepare for the first-ever attempted solo flight across the Pacific.

and, on November 21, obtained an airplane radio permit from the Federal Communications Commission (FCC). News of the permit—for use "only for communication with ships and coastal stations when in flight over the sea"—sparked speculation in the press that she was planning a flight over the Pacific, but as usual, Amelia and G. P. quickly tamped down the rumors. Amelia, G. P. stated, was on a lecture tour in California and had simply obtained an FCC license to pursue her personal interest in "experimental radio work."

Days later, they had disastrous news. On November 26, after G. P. had shut down the house in Rye and moved to Manhattan, a raging boiler fire broke out that destroyed much of the sixteen-room home, including valuable paintings, family silver, and nearly all of the personal papers and poems that Amelia had saved since childhood. The structural damage alone was estimated at $75,000.

G. P. made plans to rebuild, but his immediate concern was launching Amelia's record-setting Pacific flight. In a few weeks he was back in California, and on December 22, he and Amelia left for Honolulu aboard the ocean liner *Lurline*, accompanied by Paul Mantz and the Vega, which was lashed to the deck. The trip, they insisted to the press, was just a vacation, though it was possible, G. P. hinted, that Amelia might choose to fly back to California.

Pacific flights, and their dangers, had been all over the headlines. In early November, Australian aviator Sir Charles Kingsford-Smith, along with a navigator, had safely flown the twenty-four-hundred mile stretch from Honolulu to Oakland. A month later, however, pilot Charles Ulm and two crewmates had vanished flying the same hazardous expanse of water over the Pacific Ocean. On December 11, the United States government called off a week-long search for the flyers involving nearly sixty army, navy, and coast guard airplanes and surface vessels. There was considerable criticism of the expensive hunt, and on December 29, two days after the *Lurline* docked in Hawaii, the *Honolulu Star-Bulletin* publicly issued a stern warning to Amelia. If she intended to fly solo from Hawaii to the mainland, the paper declared, "responsible authorities should stop her from doing it." If she failed in the dangerous attempt, the editors warned, "the ghastly Ulm search would be repeated, probably with more enthusiasm, which in the air means greater risks and probable loss of life."

Opposite G. P. and Amelia at home in Rye, New York

Below Her Lockheed Vega is loaded onto the liner *Lurline* for the trip to Hawaii, where she planned to take off on her Pacific solo.

Hawaii to California. "Fifty per cent of the planes that have started on the transpacific hop have not come through," he warned, and "a flight at this season of the year, when storms sweep down suddenly from the Aleutian Islands, would be especially dangerous." As speculation continued, some editors were calling her proposed flight a stunt, and other critics accused her of selling her soul to the Hawaiian sugar interests. In the face of the controversy, her sponsors got skittish and wanted to pull out, but Amelia personally confronted them for being spineless. Wearing jodhpurs and a leather jacket, she strode into a meeting they were holding at the Royal Hawaiian Hotel. "Gentlemen," she scolded, "there is an aroma of cowardice in this air." The rumors were "trash," she declared, but "whether you live in fear or defend your integrity is your decision. I have made mine. I intend to fly to California within this next week, with or without your support." She won over her backers and retained their funding, but the "barrage of belittlement," she acknowledged, was exacting a painful and serious personal cost.

It did not, however, weaken her resolve and determination. On Friday, January 11, at 4:45 in the afternoon, she took off in her Vega from muddy Wheeler Field and flew east over the Pacific Ocean, heading for California. Equipped with a radio telephone, she stayed in two-way voice communication with shore stations and ships during the flight. She even heard G. P. speaking to her, clear as a bell, over the airwaves from radio station KGU in Honolulu. Hearing his voice, she recalled, was a high point of the trip, as was the stunning clarity of the night sky over the Pacific Ocean. Millions of stars seemed near enough to touch, and there were no words for the beauty of it, she later wrote—"only a thrill—the vibrant, icy, numbing waves that rise like a message from the soul to

The criticism was unexpected and stinging. G. P. once or twice caught a strange look in Amelia's eyes, "a kind of anxiety," he remembered, "that was not normal to her." She tried to relax, sunning and taking long walks at the Waikiki home of Chris Holmes, the Fleischman yeast heir, who had invited them to stay at his well-staffed estate. They were living "like kings," Amelia reported, while Paul readied the Vega at Wheeler Field, but press sniping and accusations continued. In the first week of January, Frank Flynn, a member of the National Aeronautic Association, publicly urged Amelia to abandon any plans to fly solo from

mind . . . " She faced challenges, too, battling blindly through squalls and fog, her eyes blurry with tears from air blasting onto her face through a broken vent. Finally, after 18 hours, 16 minutes over open water, she set down her Vega at Oakland Airport, where ten thousand jubilant fans had been waiting for hours. As she slowed her propellers to a stop, she threw open her cockpit and smiled, tired and red-eyed, at the cheering crowds. This had been her "hardest flight," Amelia said, because of the "mental hazard" of all the criticism she had endured. She was exhausted and wanted to sleep more than anything, but she had no plans, she

THRILL

On my flight from Hawaii, I had been so busy with my motor, fuel supply, instruments and radio that I had given no thought to myself or the world around me. When the moon set, there came a lull. I looked out upon the night. The horizon was so low that there seemed to be stars beneath me! I knew it was an illusion, but it was real. I seemed to be peering over the edge of the black ocean--- peering at the stardrift from below. All of my life there had been stars above. Now there were stars beneath! Beauty and vision had come together. I could not cry it aloud. There were no words for it-- only a thrill-- the vibrant, icy, numbing waves that rise like a message from the soul to mind, "I know. I know."

I never use the word, thrilling, to describe trivial sensations. I seldom use it because only a few things are thrilling in a lifetime. Sometimes one thrills with sudden awareness of beauty so awesome and rare that one trembles with the discovery. Sometimes one thrills to self-revelation, to the light that breaks after years of darkness, to sudden consciousness of hidden powers, the challenge of the future and the freedom of self.

announced, to give up long-distance flying—"not while there's life in the old horse yet," she added with a weary smile.

Amelia was now at the pinnacle of her career—the first person, man or woman, who had ever flown solo across both the Atlantic and Pacific oceans. President Roosevelt was full of praise, saying she had "scored again" and "shown even the 'doubting Thomases' that aviation is a science which cannot be limited to men only." Eleanor Roosevelt quickly cabled congratulations, adding "am so relieved to have you back safely." The achievement, the first lady remarked, was "just grand," and she invited Amelia and G. P. to stay at the White House when they came to Washington.

Amelia was now an iconic world figure, an "established heroine," and she and Eleanor Roosevelt were the two most famous women in the United States. G. P., however, soon found himself without a job and at loose ends. He quit Paramount in March 1935 and was "in a state," Amelia wrote, "trying to decide what alley he will run down." In the meantime, he focused all his energy on Amelia's career, wasting no time in organizing another highly publicized, potentially profitable long-distance flight.

At a reception in New York, Amelia had met the consul general of Mexico, who invited her to fly to his country on a goodwill visit; it was "the first time," she said, that she'd "ever been asked

was hoping to make the seventeen-hundred-mile trip without a break, but a seed or insect flew in her eye when she was over Mexico, and she came down in Nopala—where crowds of cowboys, women, and children, she said, "strangely knew who I was" and helped her get her bearings for Mexico City. There, after a warm welcome by thousands, she and G. P., were lavishly honored and entertained for eighteen days.

Meanwhile, they made preparations for her attempted nonstop solo flight back to the United States. Mexico City was seventy-five hundred feet above sea level, and the thin air at that high altitude would seriously reduce the lifting power of her heavy Vega. To take off safely carrying a full load of explosive fuel, Amelia would need a much longer runway, so the Mexican government constructed a special three-mile-long airstrip for her in a dry lake bed outside the city. There were other perils ahead too. Amelia wanted to fly as directly as possible from Mexico City to the New York

Below A Mexican postage stamp—overprinted with the words "Amelia Earhart Vuelo de Buena Voluntad, Mexico 1935"—commemorating her goodwill visit and solo flight from Mexico City to the U.S. in 1935.

anywhere." On March 17, barely two months after her Pacific crossing, she announced that she would make the first nonstop twenty-one-hundred-mile solo flight from Mexico City to New York. To finance the costly trip, the Mexican government agreed to issue nearly eight hundred special airmail stamps overprinted with a message commemorating her historic flight. Amelia would carry several hundred of the stamps, worth up to $100 each, on her flight back to the United States to sell to collectors.

On April 19, she flew her Vega on another record flight, from California to Mexico City, where she planned to rendezvous with G. P. and make the official rounds of her goodwill visit. Amelia

area. That meant crossing the Gulf of Mexico, a hazardous 700-mile stretch of open water—"half an Atlantic," according to Wiley Post, a celebrated pilot who had flown solo around the world and as high as 50,000 feet wearing a pressure suit. Wiley urged Amelia not to do it—it was too risky—but that only made her more eager than ever to make the flight. If Wiley Post, "the man who had braved every sort of hazard in his stratosphere flying," considered a flight across the Gulf too dangerous, Amelia said, she could hardly wait to take on the challenge.

On the morning of May 9, 1935, she took off, without incident, from the specially built runway into the thin air of Mexico City and headed out over the Gulf of Mexico. Fourteen hours later, Amelia circled gracefully over Newark Airport and made a perfect three-point landing, cutting her engine as three thousand fans rushed through police cordons onto the field. This time, there were no signs of fatigue. The flight, Amelia reported, had not been especially interesting, but she had managed to set another speed record for women.

She was now such a legend that a thousand people came out to the airport just to peer at her

Vega, and there was hardly time for Amelia to take a breath. Although G. P. had predicted she'd have "a few months of domesticity" after the Mexican flight—so she could add "home touches" to their newly rebuilt house in Rye—Amelia, instead, was dashing nonstop from city to city. From May 23 to May 30, she was in Chicago, Washington, Atlanta, New York, and Indianapolis, where she served as

the first woman referee of the Indy 500 road race. Three days later, she made her first parachute jump, along with Gene Vidal, before traveling west for the rest of June on a packed lecture schedule.

Since the beginning of the year, Amelia had flown across the Pacific, then to Mexico and back, followed by breakneck rounds of public events and appearances. By the end of the month, she was so stressed and fatigued that her old sinus infection kicked up and she had to check into Cedars of Lebanon Hospital in Los Angeles for an operation.

Left Poster for an event celebrating Amelia's visit in the Plaza de Toros in Mexico City

Right Program for a concert given in her honor by the Mexican National Conservatory of Music

She and G. P. were still hoping to get back to Wyoming, but Amelia was laid low again in early July with backaches, headaches, and a painful infection in her lungs.

She loved the sunshine and warmth in Los Angeles and wanted to stay there, but G. P. was resisting the idea of leaving the East Coast, even though they were too busy to spend time at the house in Rye and were renting it out. On a whim, however, at the end of July, G. P. suggested they buy a small house in North Hollywood, in Toluca Lake. Just two days later, they owned the property and were making major plans to expand and remodel the home.

Amelia was also busy brainstorming business ideas. Her investment in Boston & Maine Airways had been paying off, and she was now

planning to partner with Paul Mantz in a new flying school, an airplane charter business, and "all kinds of things" that could bring in additional income. She was also thinking, reading, and seeing friends—taking time off from being a personality, she said, and just "being a person." Every once

Above In 1935, Amelia was named the first woman referee of the Indy 500 road race.

Left Her Vega, surrounded by adoring fans, in 1935

in a while, she explained, "it's good to stop and look around and find out what the whole thing means."

Her quiet time away, however, didn't last long. At the end of August, Amelia entered the Bendix, flying her Vega, with Paul and a mechanic aboard, in the twenty-two-hundred-mile sprint from L.A. to Cleveland. She and Paul had decided to enter the race at the last minute; Amelia never thought she had "much chance of winning," she told the press, but she decided to go "for the ride anyway" and finished fifth. By the end of September, she was back to her old pace, running hard, she said, on a "very strenuous lecture tour." In October alone, she wrote Gene, she spoke twenty-nine times, at $300 a talk, "usually driving at night," she told him, "and sleeping during the day."

In early November, Amelia took on yet another job, as a "woman's career consultant" and technical aeronautical adviser at Purdue University in Indiana. Purdue's president, Edward C. Elliott, wanted to improve career opportunities for women, and he thought that Amelia would be an ideal role model for Purdue's eight hundred coeds. He had met her at a conference in September 1934, and soon after, at the Coffee House Club in New York City, as Amelia sat on a couch, "her feet tucked up under her like a little girl," Elliott asked her if she'd

Opposite Amelia jumps from a parachute training tower in a publicity stunt organized by G. P.

Left In Los Angeles, they get the keys to their new Toluca Lake home, which they planned to share with Amelia's mother, Amy, after renovations.

like to become a visiting Purdue faculty member. Amelia liked the idea, and they soon agreed that she'd spend a few weeks a year at the university, at a salary of $2,000. Amelia would have a free hand "ventilating" her philosophy about careers for women, and she'd also serve as an adviser in aeronautics, since Purdue taught practical aviation and was the only university in the country with its own hundred-acre airport. After Elliott formally announced Amelia's appointment on June 2, 1935, the number of entering women freshman jumped 50 percent.

In 1935, Amelia advised and inspired hundreds of coeds as a "women's career counselor" and technical adviser at Purdue University in Indiana.

In November, Amelia spent three weeks on the Purdue campus, coaching coeds on subjects including career choices, marriage, and discrimination. According to one student, a major in electrical engineering, Amelia explained the obstacles in the path of women who wanted to go into a "man's field." She was encouraging, though; she "didn't see why, if a woman had special talents along that line, she couldn't go out and show 'em." The students loved her warm, accessible style. Amelia slept in the women's dorm and took her meals with students in the dining hall, often with her elbows on the table as she listened to their conversations. She created a stir one evening when she showed up for dinner in flying togs instead of ladylike attire, and she scandalized faculty wives by walking around town wearing masculine slacks. After hours, girls loved

wandering into her room in pajamas and slippers just to chat about life, and they admired the long hours Amelia always put in. "One night," a student recounted,

I was sitting in my room studying, and Miss Earhart stuck her head in the door and asked if she could borrow my pen. She said, 'I'll bring it back in just a sec,' just like any girl would do. I guess I couldn't keep it to myself because, when she did bring it back, there was a bunch of girls in my room—just to get another look at her. But really, you know, I don't think she gets enough sleep. She's terribly busy. I often hear her typewriter clear up to midnight.

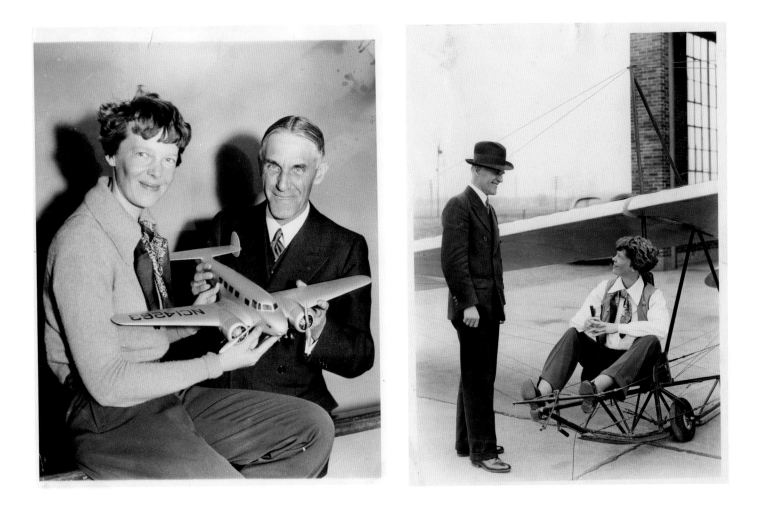

She was having a grand time at Purdue, and she was having an impact. At a dinner party that fall, President Elliott asked her how they might be able to collaborate further. Amelia was planning to retire her Vega, "the old family bus," and she told him she had an idea for a "flying laboratory" that could explore the effects of aviation on human beings. The "laboratory," in fact, would be a brand new plane—the best, fastest, and first fully pressurized multiengine airplane in the world. The state-of-the-art aircraft, the Lockheed Electra, could fly faster than two hundred miles an hour, with a top range up to four thousand miles. The Purdue Research Foundation soon agreed to finance the purchase of the Electra for Amelia, offering her

$50,000 to fund the pursuit of "pure and applied aeronautical research" in her flying lab.

Amelia would soon have "a new airyplane to play with," she told her mother—a plane so powerful, she realized, that she'd be able to take on the hardest, longest, most dangerous record attempt of her career.

Above left and right Edward C. Elliott, Purdue's president, wanted to collaborate with Amelia on aeronautical research, including the construction of a powerful new "flying laboratory."

6

THE LAST GRAND ADVENTURE

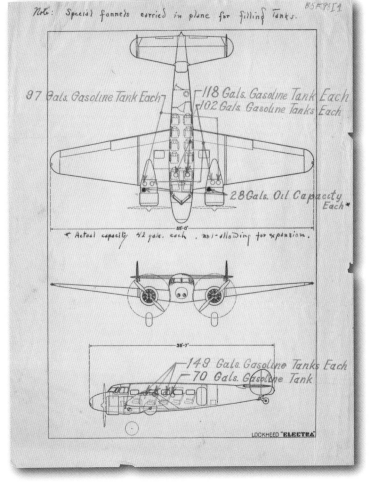

Note: Special funnels carried in plane for filling Tanks.

97 Gals. Gasoline Tank Each

118 Gals. Gasoline Tank Each
102 Gals. Gasoline Tanks Each

28 Gals. Oil Capacity Each *

* Actual capacity 42 gals. each, not-allowing for expansion.

149 Gals. Gasoline Tanks Each
70 Gals. Gasoline Tank

LOCKHEED "ELECTRA"

Flying around the world was the ultimate challenge. Only a handful of pilots had ever succeeded. In 1924, four American army aviators hopscotched around the earth in two biplanes, a trip that took them nearly six months to complete. In 1931, Wiley Post and his navigator Harold Gatty flew the shortest route around the world, near the Arctic Circle, making the complete circuit in just eight and a half days. Two years later, Wiley repeated his globe-girdling, top-of-the-world flight—solo, this time—and shaved nearly an entire day off his own record. There were few spectacular "firsts" left for world-conquering pilots—except for a flight around the earth at the equator, the longest route, a passage that would require a hazardous crossing of the entire Pacific.

Ever since she was a child, Amelia had been captivated by "imaginary journeys full of fabulous perils." For years she had been hankering to make a round-the-world flight; it would be a "fling," she told Louise Thaden, a risky and romantic exploit she wanted to attempt for "purely selfish reasons." A globe-circling flight, especially one at the equator, would be a "shining adventure," Amelia explained, "beckoning with new experiences, added knowledge of flying, of peoples—of myself." Now, with a powerful new plane at her disposal, Amelia's dream of seeing "this very interesting world at its waistline" could start coming true.

With Purdue's financing in place—through its newly established Amelia Earhart Fund for Aeronautical Research—Lockheed started work on her dream ship, a sophisticated, silvery metal monoplane specially engineered for long-distance flying. Amelia's new low-winged Electra, ordered in March 1936,

Opposite Amelia and her Lockheed Electra

Above A diagram of her brand new "flying laboratory"

was outfitted with two 550-horsepower Wasp engines, extra gas tanks boosting its fuel capacity to twelve hundred gallons, de-icing appliances, a special roof hatch for navigation, a radio "homing" device, a two-way radio telephone system, and a Sperry Gyro-Pilot, an automatic pilot device that Wiley Post had used on his solo flight around the world. In late July, just in time for her thirty-ninth birthday, the Electra was hers, and for weeks after

CITY OF NEW YORK
MUNICIPAL AIRPORTS
NO.1 FLOYD BENNETT FIELD · NO. 2 NORTH BEACH
EAST RIVER SEAPLANE BASES   WALL STREET — 31ST STREET
F. H. LaGUARDIA   JOHN McKENZIE
      MAYOR   COMMISSIONER OF DOCKS

She tested the Electra by flying it from Floyd Bennett Field to Los Angeles in the 1936 Bendix race.

that, Amelia "wore a groove" flying up and down the West Coast between San Francisco and southern California, learning to pilot the sophisticated plane with its complex controls.

After training for over a month with the help of Paul Mantz, she decided to give her new plane a shakedown by entering it in the Bendix

competition on September 4. It was a frightening flight. Soon after she took off from Floyd Bennett Field, the roof hatch flew open, nearly sucking Amelia and her co-pilot, Helen Richey, right out of the cockpit. They struggled for two hours before they could jam it closed, and they took only fifth place in L.A., but still, they had reason for pride. The first-place winners, for the first time in the history of the Bendix, were two women flyers, Louise Thaden and Blanche Noyes, and a third woman pilot, Laura Ingalls, soloed her plane to a second-place finish.

Rumors, meanwhile, were spreading that Amelia was planning to make a globe-circling flight. It was nonsense, she said; she merely expected to "hop here and there around the world" in her new flying lab, doing practical research on fuel consumption, communication, navigation, and human factors of fatigue and endurance. Reports of a round-the-world flight, she insisted to Amy, were just "applesauce." It would take months to plan such a trip, Amelia told her, maybe even a year. Her protests, G. P. admitted, were all "a white lie" to fend off the problems and pressures of advance publicity. In truth, plans for Amelia's world flight were already well under way.

While Amelia traveled, lectured, and learned how to master the Electra, G. P. took charge of the venture's logistical planning. It was an immense task. The twenty-seven-thousand-mile route she intended to fly would take her from Oakland to Honolulu, across the Pacific to New Guinea and northern Australia, then via South Asia to Arabia and the west coast of Africa, across the South Atlantic to Brazil, then northward and back home to the United States. G. P. pored over maps, weather data, and detailed reports on landing, servicing, and emergency facilities, plotting where to ship caches of fuel, oil, and spare parts and

Vincent Bendix congratulates Louise Thaden and Blanche Noyes, the first women pilots to win the grueling cross-country competition.

arrange expert mechanical support for repairing and maintaining the plane. He also had to secure official permission from every country Amelia planned to land in or fly over along the way. For help with these intricate diplomatic arrangements, he turned to Amelia's great friend and supporter, Eleanor Roosevelt. At the first lady's instruction, her secretary advised the country's chief of protocol "to take care of the things [G. P.] wished done in the State Department . . . She is sure you will be *very* nice to him."

Gene Vidal, in his government job at the renamed federal Bureau of Air Commerce, was also a crucial connection. In charge of civil air navigation and regulations, he was well-positioned and willing to provide key access to information on navy landing facilities in Honolulu and weather data over the Pacific Ocean. In the fall of 1936, the personal bond, too, between Gene and Amelia had grown closer than ever. Gene and his wife had divorced in 1935, and their son, Gore, born ten years earlier, recalled that Amelia was a very important person in his young life. She visited him when he was sick, Gore remembered, and he had longed, as a child, for Amelia to marry his father and become his stepmother. Gore and Amelia used to show each other poems they had written, and Amelia often shared her poetry with Gene, too, before she submitted it to magazines under an assumed name. Gene and Amelia were

Netherland Plaza
Cincinnati, Ohio
NATIONAL HOTEL MANAGEMENT CO · INC
RALPH HITZ · PRESIDENT

Telephone Main 3800

HOTELS NEW YORKER, LEXINGTON, NEW YORK; BOOK-CADILLAC, DETROIT; RITZ-CARLTON, ATLANTIC CITY · VAN CLEVE, DAYTON

Amelia penned this draft of a love poem, perhaps for Eugene Vidal.

Gene always insisted that his relationship with Amelia was "simply professional," but there's evidence it was much more than that. Gene carried a photo of Amelia in his wallet, and when his sister visited his bachelor apartment, she found a silver hairbrush, monogrammed with the initials "A.E." and threaded with coils of Amelia's curly blond hair. Amelia was deeply in love with Gene, according to Gore, and she may have captured the passion she felt for him in several poems G. P. discovered after the fire at Rocknoll. He assumed that Amelia had composed them "for no audience but herself," but she may, instead, have written them for and about Gene:

To touch your hand or see your face, today
Is joy. Your casual presence in a room
Recalls the stars that watched us as we lay.

I mark you in the moving crowd
And see again those stars
A warm night lent us long ago.
We loved so then—we love so now.

Another fragment reads:

I have seen your eyes at dawn beloved
Dark with sleep
And lying on your breast—have watched
The new day creep

Into new depths, putting aside old shadows
Spun by night
To show again the lovely living colors
Of your sunlit sight

I would cry my joy to the world uncontrol-
lably . . .
The mountain tops of love I've known

so intimate that for years he had been buying her men's underwear, which Amelia was too embarrassed to go out and purchase herself. Men's shorts were undoubtedly more comfortable under slacks than women's lingerie of the 1930s, and they probably made it easier to urinate, like other women pilots on long-distance flights, using a funnel and pail.

If there was any doubt about the intensity of Amelia's feelings for Gene, they were fully on display in mid-September, when his job with the Department of Commerce was suddenly threatened. Word came down that the Bureau of Air Commerce was going to be reorganized; Gene would be fired, along with his two assistant directors, and a lawyer would be taking charge of the agency. Amelia, Gene's defender and champion, wasted no time rushing to his rescue. She had promised to campaign for President Roosevelt's reelection, and on September 15, 1936, she sent Eleanor an impassioned telegram:

MRS. FRANKLIN D. ROOSEVELT
THE WHITE HOUSE.
I AM WIRING YOU CONCERNING A MEAN
AND UNFORTUNATE INSTANCE OF POLITI-
CAL SCHEMING BECAUSE OF MY PROMISE
TO YOU TO JOIN THE NEW YORK STATE
AUTOMOBILE CARAVAN NEXT WEEK AND
ISSUE A STATEMENT FOR THE NATIONAL
COMMITTEE. AVIATION IS MY VOCATION
AND AVOCATION. I SHOULD RATHER
HELP THE INDUSTRY PROGRESS THAN
PROGRESS MYSELF. THUS I FEEL THE PRE-
EMPTORY DISMISSAL OF THE DIRECTOR
OF AIR COMMERCE AND TWO ASSISTANTS
SUBSTITUTING LEGALLY TRAINED INDI-
VIDUAL FOR ONE OF PRACTICAL EXPERI-
ENCE IS ALMOST A CALAMITY. THERE IS
LITTLE USE OF MY TRYING TO INTEREST
OTHERS IN THE PRESIDENT'S CAUSE
WHEN MY HEART IS SICK WITH THE
KNOWLEDGE THAT AN INDUSTRY CAN
BE JEOPARDIZED AND AN INDIVIDUAL'S
CAREER BLASTED BY WHAT SEEMS A PER-
SONAL FEUD. MAY I HOPE THAT BEFORE
ANY SCALPS ARE ATTACHED TO ANYONE'S

BELT THE PRESIDENT WILL PERSONALLY
ASCERTAIN THE TRUE SITUATION FROM
MR. VIDAL. SURELY ONE DAY'S NOTICE OF
DISMISSAL CAN ONLY RESULT IN CONFU-
SION IN A BUREAU LONG A TARGET OF
ATTACK AND IS POOR REWARD FOR LOYAL
SERVICE. PLEASE BELIEVE THIS MESSAGE
IS NOT INSTIGATED BY ONE OF THOSE AF-
FECTED INSTEAD IT IS SENT PERSONALLY
AND SOLELY IN THE INTERESTS OF FAIR
PLAY. IF YOU WOULD LIKE TO QUESTION
ME PLEASE WIRE INSTRUCTING WHEN I
MAY TELEPHONE YOU.

Gore Vidal, at age ten, looks over an airplane with his father, Gene.

Vidal served as director of the Bureau of Air Commerce from 1933 until early 1937.

HELPFULNESS IN THE MATTER ABOUT
WHICH I WIRED YOU. AM INFORMED OUT-
COME NOW PROMISES TO BE SATISFACTORY
TO VIDAL WHOSE LOYALTY MERITS THE
FAIR TREATMENT WHICH YOUR INTERESTS
SECURING. I AM SURE YOU UNDERSTAND
I WAS ACTUATED BY DESIRE TO SERVE THE
INDUSTRY, THE INDIVIDUAL AND THE
ADMINISTRATION.
GRATEFULLY, AMELIA EARHART

On September 19, Amelia kept her word and endorsed President Roosevelt "because of his social conscience," pledging to take an active role in his campaign. The following week, she joined the Democratic women's caravan in upstate New York, stumping for FDR's reelection. As Gene promptly informed the Democratic National Committee, Amelia also promised to promote the president's candidacy in twenty-eight lectures she was scheduled to deliver that autumn.

Gene had depended on Amelia, and she was depending on him to help smooth the official logistics for her round-the-world flight. That fall he and the Roosevelts offered Amelia extraordinary support for her globe-circling adventure, especially in preparations for her Pacific crossing. A key challenge was determining how she could make the long leg over the vast Pacific Ocean west of Honolulu. Tokyo, the closest landing facility, was thirty-nine hundred miles away, farther than the Electra, with its four-thousand-mile maximum range, could realistically fly. Amelia would have to find a way to take on more gasoline as she crossed the Pacific, and she began exploring the possibility of an aerial refueling. On November 10, she wrote directly to the president about her "confidential plans for a world flight," asking him to help her win navy cooperation for "a possible refueling over Midway

The first lady, who was so attached to Amelia that she kept a copy of her poem "Courage" in her desk drawer, passed on the wire to Franklin. He, too, was exceptionally fond of Amelia and "burst out laughing" when he read her ardent defense. The next day, he cancelled the bureau's reorganization; Gene's job was safe. A day later, Amelia sent a message of thanks to Eleanor for her crucial assistance:

MRS. FRANKLIN ROOSEVELT.
THANK YOU SINCERELY FOR YOUR

Island." FDR, in a handwritten note, instructed the chief of naval operations to "Do what we can and contact Mr. Putnam." The navy promptly approved Amelia's plan, provided she got special training in aerial refueling and paid the $2,000 cost of the operation. A midair refueling would solve the problem of the Electra's range—but if Amelia stayed in the air for the entire distance across the Pacific, she would be flying for at least twenty-four hours over open water without a break, an almost impossibly dangerous scenario.

Fortunately, Gene and the Bureau of Air Commerce came up with a solution. The South Pacific was dotted with small coral islands, and one of them, Gene suggested, could be equipped with a landing strip that Amelia would be able to use as a refueling stop on her long overwater leg. The likeliest spot would be Howland Island, a tiny, barren sandspit eighteen hundred miles southwest of Honolulu. Gene's agency had been "colonizing" Howland since 1935 with a team of young Hawaiian men "for weather observations and reporting and for the clearing of emergency landing strips." The funds for runway construction, however, had been held up, so Amelia again wrote directly to the president for help, asking him to "please forgive troublesome female flyer for whom the Howland Island project is key to world flight attempt." Once again, her personal request to Roosevelt promptly paid off; money was released so construction could begin on the mid-ocean sandbar, only two miles long, half a mile wide, and two feet above the crashing Pacific surf.

At the end of November, Amelia traveled to Philadelphia with Gene and Gore to see the Army-Navy football game, and on the way back, the eleven-year-old asked her what part of the round-the-world trip worried her the most. Africa, she said; "If you got forced down in those jungles, they'd never find you." When Gore mentioned that the Pacific looked dangerously big and wet, Amelia told him that there were lots of islands and ships that were always passing by. "Wouldn't it be wonderful," she added, turning to Gene, "to just go off and live on a desert island?" Gene wasn't sold, but they talked about how you could manage to survive on an island without fresh water by making a sun-still to extract salt from seawater. Amelia didn't lack fear—that would be "subnormal," she remarked—but any anxieties she felt were overshadowed by the challenge and thrill of pushing the limits and playing, unflinchingly, for the biggest stakes.

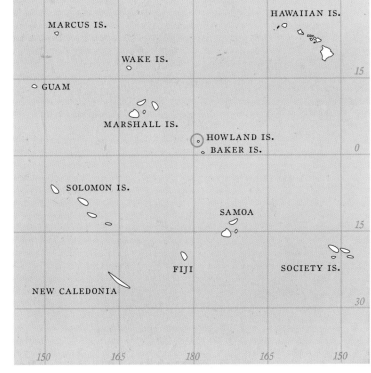

Map of the South Pacific around Howland Island, a tiny sandspit where Amelia planned to land and refuel on her flight over the ocean from Hawaii to New Guinea.

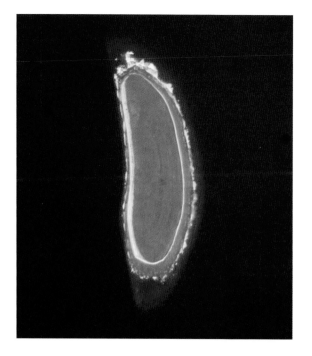

Her impulse to explore the unknown and break boundaries took a sudden, supernatural turn that December, when she stayed at the Indio, California, ranch of her good friend, aviator Jackie Cochran. The ranch, Jackie wrote, was Amelia's retreat, a place where she loved to go "streaking across the desert on horseback," planned her round-the-world flight, and built up her strength for the strenuous journey. Jackie believed she had extrasensory perception, and, though Amelia put little stock in superstitions, she and G. P. had long been fascinated by "the borderland" of psychic phenomena. For years, out of "healthy curiosity," they had "sat in on table-tappings and other experiments," and Amelia, especially, had a "fragile psychic quality," according to G. P. "some strange

The Bureau of Air Commerce built a runway for Amelia on Howland (above), an island only two miles long and half a mile wide; the remains of the runway (right) in 2008.

Amelia in 1936 with her friend, pilot and psychic Jackie Cochran, at Jackie's ranch in Indio, California.

susceptibility to conditions beyond understanding. She rarely mentioned it to friends, never discussed it publicly. But whenever AE participated in mental telepathy or other psychic experiments to further her curiosity, observers were astonished at the results."

Movie star Mae West was one witness to her psychic powers. In early 1935, when G. P. was still working for Paramount, Amelia conducted a séance for Mae, who was eager to contact the spirits of her dead parents. As participants sat around a table, Amelia directed them not to disturb it in any way; the spirits, she said, would reveal their presence by tipping the table so it tapped the floor in front of the individual they wished to contact. "Suddenly," Mae remembered, "the table began to tip in my direction" and tapped out a message from her dead father, each letter signified by a certain number of raps. Amelia was Mae's spirit guide into the mysteries of the paranormal, and the actress was so swayed by the experience that she started trying to cultivate her own psychic talents.

The next year, when Amelia and Jackie Cochran became friends, they discovered their shared interest in ESP, and their "sixth-sense notions," Jackie remembered, "had burst into full bloom." On December 15, when they learned, in

Navigator Harry
Manning and Amelia
inside the Electra in
1937

Indio, that a Western Air Express transport plane had vanished between Los Angeles and Salt Lake City, they decided to try to find the missing plane using psychic powers. Amelia asked Jackie questions about the plane's location, while Jackie identified the site in her mind's eye and talked about mountain roads and transmission lines near Salt Lake City. After Paul Mantz found the likely area on a map, Amelia took off in her plane to search for the lost wreckage and any survivors. She found nothing, but "the real shock," Jackie wrote, "came in the spring when the snow in those mountains had melted and the wreck of the transport emerged where we said it might," only two miles from the spot they had predicted.

Jackie's sixth sense, she said, gave her "vague apprehensions" about Amelia's round-the-world flight. Louise Thaden, too, had worries about the trip. Soon after the new year, in January 1937, Louise met Amelia at the Union Air Terminal in Burbank, California. As the two friends walked arm in arm into the hangar, Louise asked Amelia why she wanted to take all the risks of such a hazardous flight; "it seems to me," Louise said, that "you have everything to lose and nothing to gain." Amelia replied that she'd wanted to make the round-the-world flight for a long time. "If I bop off," she grinned, "you can carry on . . . but I'll be back." Louise, joking grimly, asked Amelia what flowers she should send to the funeral; water lilies,

Amelia thought, would be appropriate. "If I *should* bop off," she said more seriously, "it will be doing the thing I've always wanted most to do. Being a fatalist yourself, you know the man with the little black book has a date marked down for all of us when our work here is finished." Louise, a passionate aviator like Amelia, was hardly sentimental. "If your time has come to go," she mused, flying "is a glorious way in which to cross over. Smell of burning oil, the feel of strength and power beneath your hands," and "in your mind's eye the everlasting beauty and joy of flight." That beauty—"so awesome and rare that one trembles with the discovery," Amelia wrote—was the ultimate thrill, a transcendent experience, and dangers only heightened its hypnotic power.

In early 1937, plans for Amelia's world flight were falling into place. By mid-January, a Coast Guard cutter was steaming from Honolulu to Howland Island, loaded with construction equipment to build the runway she depended on for her Pacific crossing. Amelia had also chosen a navigator to guide her across the long overwater stretch. Captain Harry Manning was a merchant marine officer, a veteran ocean navigator and winner of the Congressional Medal of Honor for bravery at sea. Amelia had met him in 1928 when he was captain of the *President Roosevelt,* the ship that had carried her home across the Atlantic after the *Friendship* flight. The two of them had talked then about working together, and now, at Amelia's request, he was taking a leave of absence from a steamship line to serve as her navigator over the Pacific Ocean, from Oakland to Australia.

On February 11, in New York City, Amelia "reluctantly" announced plans for her round-the-world flight, which she said had been "smoked out" by the press. She intended to leave from Oakland the following month, fly to Honolulu,

then cross the Pacific with Captain Manning to Howland Island, Lae, New Guinea, and Darwin, Australia. From there, she would fly, solo if possible, northwest over India and Africa, then cross

the South Atlantic to Brazil. After reaching South America, Amelia planned to follow commercial air routes back to Oakland, California, completing the circle.

Weeks later, however, she was reconsidering her exclusive reliance on Harry Manning. On test flights, the double duty of serving as navigator and radio operator kept Manning "jumping around all the time," under excessive strain. The best plan,

Amelia examines her new Bendix direction finder, a homing device that took bearings on radio signals.

she thought, would be to add another crew member and split the job of navigation and radio operation. Paul Mantz recommended that she bring on Fred Noonan, a master mariner and former transport pilot who had been a navigator for Pan American Airways on its Clipper flying boat service from San Francisco to Honolulu. Although Manning was a seasoned ocean navigator, Noonan was an expert in aerial navigation, a different specialty, and had already crossed the Pacific Ocean in an airplane eighteen times. There were other issues to consider, however. Though Noonan's professional reputation was spotless, he was known to be a heavy drinker. He had a habit of going on benders, and before takeoff, a former supervisor said, he would sometimes "have to be hunted down and 'poured' aboard the airplane." Gene Vidal thought Noonan was too much of a risk, but Amelia, in the end, decided to bring him aboard. Her plan was to have Noonan fly with her to Howland Island, then return to the United States by ship, while Manning

would continue with her over the remainder of the Pacific to Port Darwin, Australia.

On March 11, Amelia and G. P. flew the Electra to Oakland, where she prepared to take off on the first leg of her round-the-world flight. While Amelia was busy taking tests for instrument flying and renewing her transport license, G. P. focused on financial and promotional deals. Short-tempered and stressed, an observer recalled, he would go "screaming through the lobby" of the airport hotel, shouting "out of the way, boys." He had already persuaded companies to donate all the gasoline, instruments, and radio equipment for the Electra, and he was scheduling well-paying rounds of lectures for Amelia after the trip. He had also been working with Gimbel's department store in New York City, which was selling specially printed collector's envelopes that Amelia would carry with her on her flight around the world. Called "first day covers," the envelopes would be postmarked en route and in Oakland on the days she departed

Before taking off on her world flight, she autographed postal envelopes, called "special covers," that she would carry and postmark on the trip and sell to collectors.

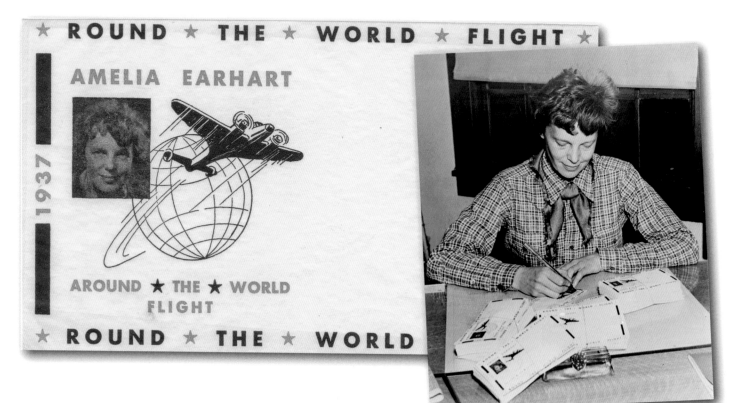

and returned. Unsigned envelopes would sell for $2.50, but those with Amelia's autograph would fetch twice that amount. To earn as much as they could from the deal, every morning in Oakland, G. P. had Amelia sign ten of the covers before she drank her orange juice and fifteen before she tucked into her eggs, then another twenty-five each night before she was able to get to bed.

Meanwhile, preparations for Amelia's arrival on tiny Howland Island were nearly finished. The government had shipped out tractors and graders. Workers then offloaded them onto pontoon rafts in dangerous, twisting surf—steering them to shore, at considerable peril, to groom the islet's new mile-long runway, the first U.S. landing field

in the South Pacific. Navy and Coast Guard vessels, too, were standing by to assist Amelia. The minesweeper *Whippoorwill* was moving into position between Honolulu and Howland, the Coast Guard cutter *Shoshone* was steaming toward the island, and the navy tug *Ontario* was heading for the 2,550-mile stretch of the Pacific between New Guinea and Howland.

Everything was in place, but stormy skies over Oakland were delaying takeoff. Finally, on March 17, there was a break in the weather. At 4:37 that afternoon, Amelia, Paul Mantz, Manning, and Noonan boarded the Electra and soared over the Golden Gate Bridge, bound for Hawaii. Amelia, hoping to conserve strength for the long

Amelia with Paul Mantz (left) and her two navigators, Fred Noonan (far right) and Harry Manning

trip ahead, piloted the plane for most of the Pacific leg, but she gave the controls to Paul for takeoff and landing. Even so, when he set down the Electra in Honolulu, after nearly sixteen hours of flying, she felt spent and exhausted. Amelia was "terribly tired," she told reporters in Honolulu. While she rested at Chris Holmes's beachfront estate, she gave Paul complete responsibility for readying the Electra for the next hop—the most dangerous one—to Howland Island, a speck "no bigger than the Cleveland airport" in the middle of the Pacific. If Amelia missed the tiny target, a reporter wrote, the result would be terrible to contemplate.

Paul and Amelia look over maps before her first round-the-world flight attempt.

There were other concerns. Paul had landed the plane hard, and the impact may have weakened the Electra's landing gear. Noonan, it seems, had started hitting the bottle in Honolulu, and Amelia was now thinking of dropping him from the Pacific flight. By March 20, however, she had resolved to continue with both navigators aboard. That morning, after they climbed into the Electra at Luke Field, Amelia gunned the motors and started racing down the runway at fifty miles an hour. Suddenly, she lost control of the plane, which started swaying uncontrollably and collapsed to the ground, skidding on its belly in a shower of sparks. The undercarriage was completely sheared off, and fuel was spraying over the wreckage, but Amelia was able to cut the switches and avoid an inferno. "Something must have gone wrong!" she shouted with a shake in her voice, as Manning and Noonan crawled out to survey the damage. The Electra, her dream ship, was broken, so badly smashed it would have to be taken apart and shipped back to Lockheed in California.

It was a devastating crash. Amelia's airplane was wrecked, and her dream of a round-the-world flight was in smoking ruins. From the very first, however, she was determined to pick up the pieces and try again. This was only a postponement, she insisted that very morning; she intended to carry through and finish the project that she had started. G. P., she said, fully backed her decision—"So long as you and the boys are O.K.," he had wired, "the rest doesn't matter . . . Whether you want to call it a day or keep going later is equally jake with me." Amelia, without question, wanted to try again, and Manning and Noonan, too, pledged to join her as soon as the Electra was repaired and ready. A few hours later, the three of them, along with Paul Mantz, boarded a steamer back to California. Shaken and tired, clinging to Paul as she rushed

up the gangplank, Amelia wouldn't talk to reporters, saying only, "I'll be back," as the liner started pulling out of port.

In pioneer flying, Amelia knew, "one has to take the rough with the smooth," and crack-ups were something she had come to expect and accept. This accident, however, was going to be staggeringly costly. Just how expensive, she and G. P. didn't yet know, but he guessed that it was going to cost "plenty." The decision to continue was probably as painful as it would have been to throw in the towel. Although G. P. and Amelia lived well, they weren't wealthy, and they had already stretched their resources to cover mounting expenses, including the movement of parts and mechanical experts all over the world to support the flight. Now, they would have to bear the additional cost of major repairs to a new, state-of-the-art, uninsured airplane. Amelia knew she was "more or less mortgaging the future," but after all, she said, "what are futures for?"

Workers examine the wreckage of Amelia's plane after she crashed at Luke Field while attempting to take off for Howland Island.

Amelia in a
reflective mood

But there were other costs, too, including a subtle, accelerating erosion of her reputation. The fact was, by 1937, Americans, as one newspaper put it, were "tired of ocean flyers, most of whose exploits are of the stunt variety." It was getting to be an old story, and the public was becoming inured to high-profile, long-distance flights. "The advance of aviation has been so constant, so pronounced," one editor stated, that even a world flight at the equator "does not amaze and startle the world as it would have a few years ago." The harshest blows came in a syndicated article by Marine Major Al Wilson. In an opinion piece printed in newspapers around the country, he accused Amelia of falsely claiming that her flight had a scientific purpose, saying it was merely a stunt that would earn her fat profits from lectures and promotional tie-ins.

In the face of these withering critiques, Amelia soldiered on. According to her old friend Hilton

Railey, she was bound and determined to resume her round-the-world flight because she had to. Amelia, he argued, "was caught up in the hero racket which compelled her to strive for increasingly dramatic records, bigger and braver feats that automatically insured the publicity necessary to the maintenance of her position as the foremost woman pilot in the world."

But there was more to her decision than maintaining her status as a heroic and romantic public figure. From the beginning, Amelia had always been daring and self-determined, and obstacles only sharpened her will to try. "When I undertake a task, over all protest and in spite of all adversity," she said, "I sometimes thrill, not with the task but with the realization that I am doing what I want to do." Amelia was unquestionably in the hero business, along with G. P., but this was a flight that she wanted to make for her own reasons. "Those dearest to me," she explained, realized that "the satisfaction of trying—so far as one can weigh such intangibles—is worth whatever price the trial may cost." Amelia wanted to finish what she had started; this trip, however, would be her final adventure. When she got back from the round-the-world flight, Amelia, nearing forty, wanted to "settle down to a normal life" in southern California. Although she would always continue to fly, this would be her last major, record-breaking attempt.

She couldn't wait to get started, but she was also thinking of making a few major changes. She had doubts about Manning's skills at high-speed celestial navigation, and at Jackie Cochran's suggestion, she decided to test them. When she got back to California, she flew him in circles over the Pacific to get him disoriented, then asked him to plot a course back to Los Angeles. Manning wasn't able to do it, so she dropped him from the flight and, on the advice of G. P. and Paul Mantz,

planned to continue on her second attempt with Noonan alone.

There were other important adjustments. Amelia was aiming to take off again in May, two months later than originally planned; as a result, she'd be running into a different set of weather conditions around the world. She wanted to fly over the Caribbean and Africa before the rains, so she decided to reverse her planned course and fly from west to east. Although winds would be more favorable in that direction, she would need to make the most dangerous part of the flight—the long haul between New Guinea and Howland Island—at the end of the trip instead of the beginning. As a result, Noonan would accompany her during the entire journey. Her new flight plan would also require new arrangements and clearances from every country—a task that had been challenging before but was now exponentially more difficult because Gene Vidal had recently resigned from the Bureau of Air Commerce. This time, G. P. would be taking the lead in all the complicated logistics without Gene and his government connections to grease the wheels.

He and Amelia also desperately needed to raise money. "Picking up the pieces" and financially "starting again," G. P. acknowledged, was "an almost superhuman task." In addition to paying $25,000 for the plane's repair, they had to lay out huge amounts for new flight plans and logistical arrangements. To help raise the money, Amelia went hat in hand to aviation publicist Harry Bruno, who had handled public relations for luminaries like Lindbergh and Byrd. "I don't know how it happened," Amelia told him, "but I guess I'm all washed up." Amelia, Bruno recalled, was "an unhappy girl," and together they phoned G. P. to find out how much cash she had to come up with. The total, G. P. answered, was $30,000. It was a large sum, equivalent to nearly $500,000 today, but with Bruno's help, Amelia and G. P. were able to raise more than that from donors including Richard Byrd and Floyd Odlum, Jackie Cochran's husband and a wealthy businessman.

Meanwhile, Amelia was penning another book, entitled *World Flight*, which she planned to complete on her return based on notes from the trip. G. P. was also rescheduling her appearances and lectures, and Gimbel's was promoting a second issue of special covers that Amelia would carry with her, along with the original envelopes, on her

second world-flight attempt. She and G. P. were cobbling together the money to finance the flight, but the pressures of the venture were taking a toll. G. P., Elinor Smith guessed, was "terrified of financial disaster," and his "nerves were snapping." He had always been a difficult person to deal with. Jackie Cochran and Marian Stabler, Amelia's old friend, disliked him for his dismissive rudeness, and many others had been stunned by his disrespectful attitude and angry outbursts. Amelia had always, publicly, made the best of their "amiable partnership," and at times they had seemed to be very close. Still, Gene Vidal was certain, according to Gore, that Amelia "deeply disliked her husband," and with the added stress and financial pressure, they were going through an especially bad time.

Compounding those strains, there were physical issues—Amelia seems to have stopped menstruating. Gene believed that she was going through early menopause, but Amelia, it appears, suspected there might be another cause. One morning that spring, she had coffee with a young man who was doing a stint as her official photographer. When he asked Amelia what she wanted to do after the world flight, she told him that she thought she might be pregnant, and when she got back, she added, she was planning to be "just a woman."

Soon after, on May 19—almost two months to the day since her dramatic crash—Amelia's Electra was repaired and ready. Two days later, she flew the rebuilt Lockheed up the West Coast to Oakland. From there, accompanied by Noonan, G. P., and a mechanic, she took off on the first transcontinental leg of her second world flight attempt. There was no public

Amelia takes off from Oakland Airport in her Electra.

announcement; the hop would be a shakedown to test the Electra and make sure that everything was in good working order. That evening she landed the plane in Tucson, Arizona, where one of the engines backfired and burst into flames. Fortunately, there was only minor damage, and the next morning they flew on to New Orleans for an overnight stop. Women pilots, G. P. joked, seemed to pop up everywhere, "from under stones," and that night they had dinner with a Ninety-Niner and air racer named Edna Gardner. Amelia, Gardner remembered, was tired and pale and saying something at the table about her radio when G. P. suddenly laid into her: "You had a chance to change. It's too late now," he scolded; "stop your sniveling." Amelia "wasn't sniveling" at all, Gardner remembered. "She just sat there," while G. P. was "as cruel as he could be, right in front of all of us."

The next day they continued the flight, heading over the Gulf of Mexico to Miami, where Pan

American technicians would help put the Electra in final shape for the round-the-world trip. Amelia was hoping to set off on May 30, but there were some problems with her radio transmitter. Technicians fixed the malfunction by shortening the plane's aerial antennas, and Amelia chose to make other changes to her radio system. In 1937, most ships and planes communicated exclusively in

Please know I am quite aware of the hazards of the trip. I want to do it because I want to do it. Women must try to do things as men have tried. When they fail, their failure must be but a challenge to others.

Above A note Amelia wrote explaining to G. P. why she wanted to make her round-the-world flight

Opposite G. P. and Amelia say goodbye before she takes off on the trip in June 1937.

Morse code, but Amelia and Noonan, unlike Manning, were "amateurs" at sending and receiving Morse messages. As a result, Amelia decided to remove the extra weight of equipment for code transmissions, including the Electra's two Morse code keys and a long trailing antenna, which required care and attention during takeoffs and landings. She and Noonan, unlike other pilots, planned to communicate by voice radio alone. Their radio skills, in general, were exceptionally weak; Amelia had been so busy, in fact, that she'd only received an hour's formal training in how to operate her plane's communication system.

In Miami, now, she had a little time to go fishing and reflect on her future with reporter Carl Allen, who was covering her flight for the *New York Herald Tribune*. Amelia asked him what he thought her odds were for completing the trip; his guess was fifty-fifty, and she had "a feeling," she admitted, that she might not make it all the way. In any case, she added, she had "just about one more good flight left in my system, and I hope this trip around the world is it." She had only one obsession, she confided to Allen, and that was a "horror of growing old—so I won't feel completely cheated," she told him, "if I fail to come back."

She was feeling relaxed, but G. P. was restless and nervous, pacing their hotel suite with an air of "pitiless determination" and a "machine-like will to overcome obstacles." His nagging, Amelia told Allen, was "driving her up the wall," and she couldn't wait to get going. Finally, in the early hours of June 1, preparations for her round-the-world flight were completed, and Amelia, Noonan, and G. P. made their way before dawn to Miami's Municipal Airport. Even at five-thirty in the morning, five hundred people gathered to watch her take off. While the Electra warmed up, she and G. P. had a quiet good-bye, holding hands with little to say as they watched the sunrise warming the grey sky. As soon as the Electra was ready, she and Noonan climbed into the plane; Amelia started the motors, and half a minute later they were on their way.

After some eight hours of flying over the Caribbean, they made their first landing, in Puerto Rico. There they retreated to the sixteen-hundred-acre estate of pilot Clara Livingston, a secluded refuge where they could relax and rest for the night without social distractions. The next morning, Amelia and Noonan pushed on, reluctantly, to South America—"trying to get to some other place," Amelia complained, "instead

of enjoying the place we'd already got to." She had made her schedule, however, "and had to abide by it." They flew over blue water, mountains, plains, and jungles to Caripito, Venezuela, and on June 3, they continued over the jungles to Paramaribo in Dutch Guiana. On the next leg, a 1,330-mile hop to Fortaleza, Brazil, Amelia crossed the equator for the first time. Noonan was planning to mark that geographic milestone by dousing her with a thermos of cold water, but he got so busy that he forgot to do it. He and Amelia were getting to know each other and becoming friends. His navigation area was in the back of the plane, and most of the time, they communicated over the noise of the engines by passing notes clipped with a clothespin to a

Above Amelia with a camera at Carapito Airport in Venezuela

Right Mechanics helping her off the plane in Carapito.

Opposite top left Amelia on her Electra in Gao, French West Africa

Opposite top right At the airport in Massawa, Eritrea

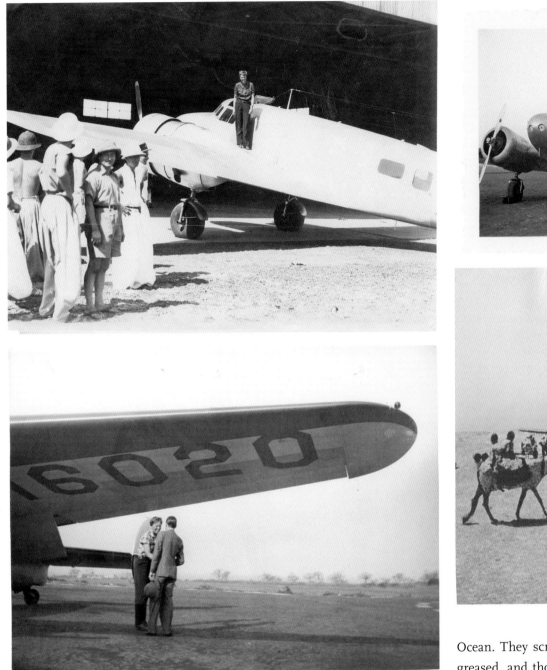

fishing pole. Sometimes, however, Noonan joined her in the cockpit, and the two of them were getting along well.

In Fortaleza, they stopped for some housekeeping before heading off over the Atlantic Ocean. They scrubbed, greased, and thoroughly checked the plane and laundered and sorted through their own meager belongings. On June 6, they flew on to Natal, on the Atlantic coast, and the following morning, at 3:15, they took off over the ocean, following a well-traveled air route. The nineteen-hundred-mile

Left Amelia arriving in Dakar, French Senegal

Above The Electra in the Sahara desert in Khartoum, Sudan

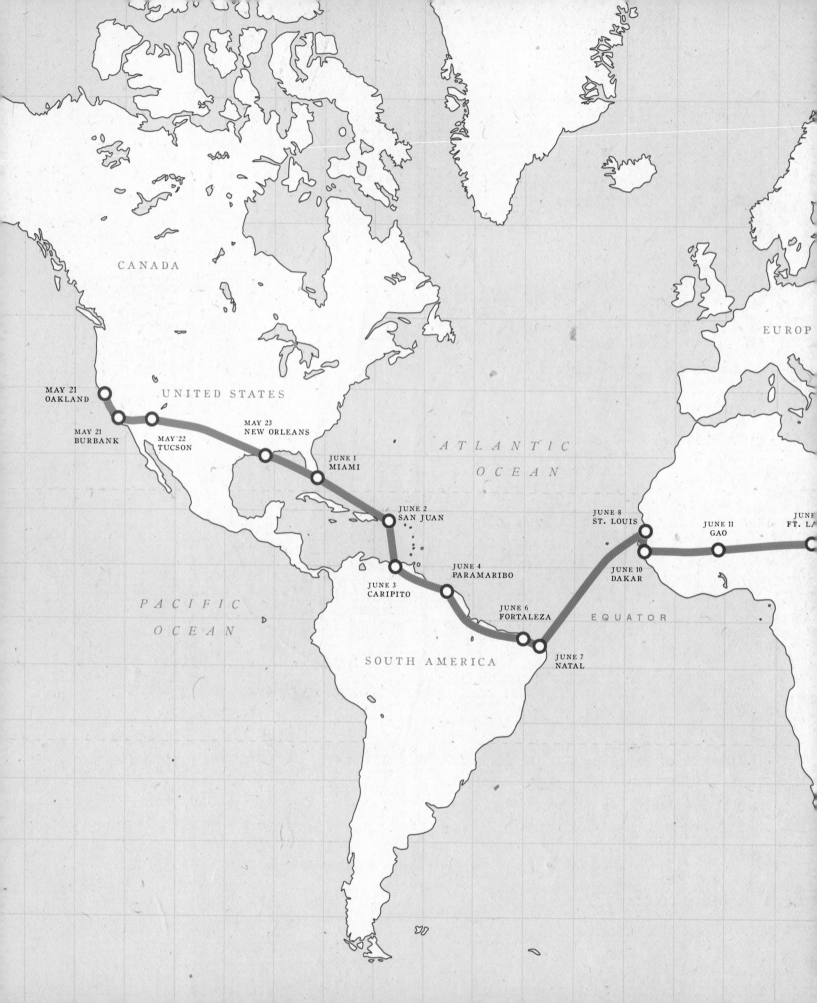

MAY 21
OAKLAND

MAY 21
BURBANK

MAY 22
TUCSON

MAY 23
NEW ORLEANS

JUNE 1
MIAMI

JUNE 2
SAN JUAN

JUNE 3
CARIPITO

JUNE 4
PARAMARIBO

JUNE 6
FORTALEZA

JUNE 7
NATAL

JUNE 8
ST. LOUIS

JUNE 10
DAKAR

JUNE 11
GAO

JUNE
FT. LA

CANADA

UNITED STATES

ATLANTIC
OCEAN

PACIFIC
OCEAN

SOUTH AMERICA

EQUATOR

EUROP

[SHOWING DEPARTURE DATES]

Amelia with her navigator, Fred Noonan

trip, Amelia wrote, was "uneventful," except for spells of "the heaviest rain I ever saw" splashing in brown sheets against the cockpit windows. Amelia was also battling nausea: "Gas fumes in plane from fueling made me sick again this morning after starting. Stomach weak I guess," she wrote in her log. Halfway across, they spotted an Air France mail plane, but Amelia and Noonan were unable to communicate with the pilot because they weren't trained or equipped to transmit in Morse code.

Some twelve hours after leaving Natal, the West African coast emerged through a thick haze. Noonan directed Amelia to make a right turn and head south to their destination of Dakar but Amelia opted to turn left instead and mistakenly landed north in the city of St. Louis, French Senegal. After spending the night, they flew the 163 miles south to Dakar, where they repaired a malfunctioning fuel gauge and checked the engines. The next day, on June 10, they took off, in the face of tornado warnings, on a seven-hour flight to Gao, a Saharan outpost on the River Niger in French West Africa. As always, Amelia wrote, she found her "calling cards" there—fifty-gallon drums of gasoline, organized by G. P. and marked with her name in big red or white letters.

Over the following days, they flew more than four thousand miles across barren, mountainous terrain so uncharted that Noonan's maps were practically useless, and he said it was easier to navigate over the open ocean. On June 13, they spotted the blue waters of the Red Sea before landing at Massawa, Eritrea, where Amelia—who, as usual, she wrote in her notes, had forgotten to eat that day—was as hungry and "hollow as a bamboo horse." Two days later, they made the first-ever two-thousand-mile nonstop flight over the coast of Arabia to Karachi, India.

The trip so far, Amelia wrote, was a hurried adventure, full of snatched impressions of people and places around landing fields filled with "the odors of baking metal, gasoline, and perspiring ground crews." Even so, she and Noonan were enjoying the journey. Amelia, Noonan wrote his wife, was "a grand person" and "the only woman flier I would care to make such a trip with because, in addition to being a fine companion she can take hardship as well as a man, and work like one." In Karachi, G. P. telephoned to check in and find out how things were going. Amelia felt "swell," she told him, "never better." It was "a grand trip," she added. "We'll do it again, together," she promised him, "some time."

G. P. might have had his doubts. He didn't mention it to Amelia, but rumors were rampant that she planned to divorce him when she got back from the trip. She was staying in touch with him,

sending him short wires and notes jotted on scraps of paper with lists of tasks she needed him to take care of. His letters to her in recent months, however, had been emotional and imploring, betraying his growing need for some reassurance:

Friday am

Hon:

. . . I'll be so happy when it's over. I want peace—and you. I'm never really content, anymore, when I'm away from you. So face the horrid likelihood of being held mighty close to me the rest of your days! Please love me a bit.

A letter G. P. wrote to Amelia in 1937

Sunday even.

Dear Hon:
. . . Hon, I miss you.
I alternate between spasms of contentment and of worry.
1. I'm so happy with you and we really do have such a swell time together, in all ways.
2. And I wish this flight wasn't hanging over us. You know I empathize fully with your ambition and will abet it. And 98% I know you'll get away with it. But we both recognize its hazards—and I love you dearly—I don't want you to run risks— and I don't want to run the risk of . . . having to go on without you—that makes me terribly sorry for myself! . . . But . . . once this is out of your hair, what a very happy, interesting time we can have. We can have it, too, should you for any reason decide to quit.

Love you lots, G.

Bottom left
Riding a camel near Karachi, India

Bottom right
Amelia with the editor of the *Rangoon Times* in Rangoon, Burma

Sunday Night

Hon dear,
. . . I have carefully analyzed our situation . . . My considered conclusion is that I love you very much and would rather fly* and work with you than with anyone I have ever encountered or could . . . Comb that out of your carefully tousled hair.

G.
*open to several interpretations, and applicable to all.

Amelia, meanwhile, was enjoying herself halfway around the world, riding camels and giving interviews to the press. On June 17, she and Noonan flew over the Central Indian plains to the Bengalese city of Calcutta, where she once again

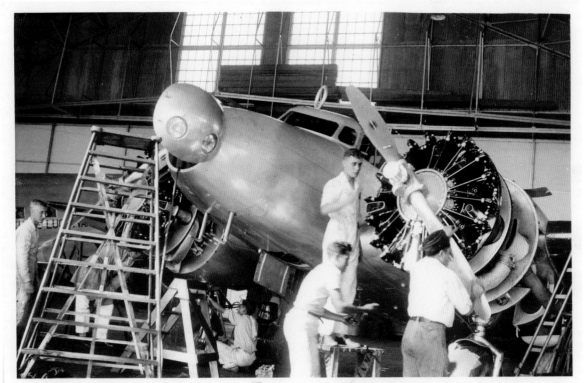

Technicians work on the Electra in Bandoeng, Java

had a telephone conversation with G. P. This time, however, her mood was profoundly different. Gene Vidal and Paul Collins were with G. P. during the call, listening in, and Paul clearly heard Amelia say that she was starting to have "personnel trouble," which they both took to be code words for Noonan's drinking. G. P. urged her to "stop the flight right away and don't take any chances," but Amelia replied that she had "only one bad hop left and I'm pretty sure I can handle the situation."

The immediate problems she faced were the dangerous, driving monsoon rains. From Calcutta, she and Noonan took off for Akyab, Burma. Although they tried to continue to Rangoon, they ran into rain so heavy that it beat the paint off the wings of the Electra— "more liquid per second," Amelia wrote, "than I thought could come out of the sky." After two hours of perilous flying, they finally gave up and turned back to Akyab. The

next morning, on June 19, they were able to reach Rangoon, spotting its sun-splashed golden pagoda from miles away. The next stops were Bangkok, Singapore, and Bandoeng, Java, where Amelia again spoke to G. P. over the phone. Now close to the end of her trip, she went over plans for her upcoming flight over the Pacific Ocean to Howland Island—discussing weather reports, navy and Coast Guard coordination, and radio frequencies that she would be using. Since she and Noonan were having problems with navigational instruments, they decided to stay in Bandoeng for six days. While mechanics inspected and repaired the plane, they took in some sightseeing, exploring an active volcano and feasting on a twenty-one-course rijsttafel in nearby Batavia.

On June 28, after an overnight stop in Koepang, Timor, they reached Port Darwin, Australia. Two days later on June 30, they landed

BANDOENG JAVA

=RADIO MISUNDERSTANDING AND PERSONNEL UNFITNESS PROBABLY WILL HOLD ONE DAY HAVE ASKED BLACK FOR FORECAST FOR TOMORROW YOU CHECK METEROLOGIST ON JOB AS FN MUST HAVE STAR SIGHTS STOP ARRANGE CREDIT IF TRIBUNE WISHES MORE STORY.

Top Noonan and Amelia in Bandoeng

Above Amelia sent this wire to G. P. from Lae, New Guinea, the day before she took off across the Pacific.

the Electra in Lae, New Guinea, their final landfall before crossing the Pacific. In one month, they had traveled twenty-two thousand miles, with another seven thousand to go before completing their long flight around the world. The most hazardous stretch, from Lae to Howland, was the very next leg, and Amelia wanted to fly it the following day, on July 1. That night, however, while she went out to dinner, Noonan settled in at the hotel

bar and "got very drunk," according to witnesses, heading to bed long after midnight. The next day, instead of flying to Howland as planned, Amelia cabled G. P.:

> RADIO MISUNDERSTANDING AND PERSON-
> NEL UNFITNESS PROBABLY WILL HOLD
> ONE DAY . . .

Again, Amelia mentioned mysterious "personnel unfitness." She knew that Noonan had gotten drunk, and as she had publicly stated, alcohol and "important" flights were a deadly mix. Commercial airlines barred pilots from having a drink twenty-four hours before a scheduled flight, and at high altitudes, Amelia believed, the effects of drinking were more lingering and pronounced. The flight from Lae to Howland would be the most important and dangerous one of her entire life; she postponed takeoff until July 2.

Part of the problem, she had told G. P., was also a "radio misunderstanding." In Port Darwin, her radio homing device hadn't been working because of a blown fuse, which she had replaced. Now Noonan was having trouble setting his chronometers—precise timekeeping devices that he needed for celestial navigation—because he wasn't able to pick up time signals on the plane's radio equipment. They were soon able to resolve the chronometer problem, and Amelia kept her eye on Noonan all day on July 1. They spent most of their time repacking the plane and eliminating everything they could possibly leave behind to save weight and fuel for the long ocean leg. In Port Darwin, they had shipped home their parachutes, which Amelia said would be useless over water, and now they were combing through their belongings to lighten the load. They also went for a sightseeing drive, with Noonan at the wheel of a borrowed truck. To Amelia, however, Lae felt like a prison; the Electra was loaded with fuel and oil, and she was anxious to go.

The next morning, at 10 a.m. local time, she and Noonan climbed into the plane and took off down the runway, carved from the jungle with a twenty-five-foot cliff over the Gulf of Huon at the end of the strip. The plane was so heavy that it sank over the gulf, flying so low, just five or six feet above the water, that its propellers were "throwing spray." But the Electra gradually rose into the morning sky over the Pacific, and they were off. The weather looked clear ahead, and U.S. Navy and Coast Guard ships were standing by to guide them the 2,556 miles across the ocean to Howland Island. The tug *Ontario* was stationed between

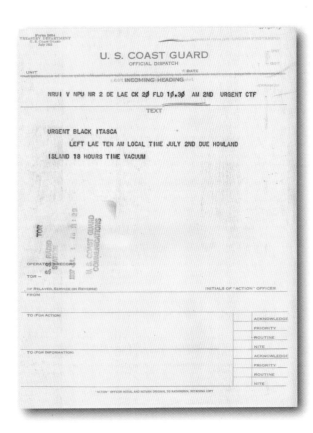

Coast Guard dispatch reporting Amelia's departure from Lae on the morning of July 2

New Guinea and Howland, and the cutter *Itasca* was positioned and waiting off Howland itself. Both vessels were tasked with staying in radio contact with Amelia and would go to her assistance, if that was necessary.

There were serious and confounding problems, however, with communication. Soon after Amelia left Lae, she started sending voice messages, using the call letters KHAQQ, but there was no evidence that she was able to receive any radio signals and establish two-way communication. The *Itasca* was expecting her to land on Howland Island at about 6:30 a.m. local time. According to the ship's radio log, Amelia broadcast the following messages as she flew her Electra over the Pacific, looking for Howland:

2:45 a.m.: Earhart voice heard, but cannot make out information.

3:45 a.m.: Earhart states that she will listen on hour and half hour on 3105 kHz.

4:53 a.m.: Earhart states "Partly Cloudy."

6:14 a.m.: Earhart wants a bearing on 3105 kHz on the hour, will whistle in microphone, about 200 miles out approximately, now whistling.

The *Itasca*, however, was not able to take a bearing on Amelia's radio transmission and started making plumes of thick, black smoke to try to guide her in.

6:45 a.m.: Earhart requests: "Please take bearing on us and report in half hour. I will make noise in mic about 100 miles out."

By now, she had been flying the Electra for over eighteen hours. More than sixty minutes after she was expected to land, she broke in:

7:42 a.m.: "KHAQQ calling Itasca we must be on you but cannot see you but gas is running low been unable to reach you by radio we are flying at 1,000 feet."

Another radio operator on Itasca recorded this message:

Earhart now says running out of gas only half hour left can't hear us at all.

There was still no two-way communication.

7:58 a.m.: "KHAQQ calling Itasca we are circling but cannot hear you go ahead on

7500 with a long count either now or on the schedule time on half hour."

Finally, Amelia heard the *Itasca's* transmission, but she wasn't able to take a bearing on the signal with her radio homing device.

8:00 a.m.: "KHAQQ calling Itasca we received your signals but unable to get a minimum. Please take bearing on us and answer 3105 with voice."

More than twenty hours after leaving Lae, Amelia and Noonan still hadn't found Howland Island. Forty-two minutes later, her voice blared through the ship's speaker "so loud" she could "hardly get any louder," stating her line of position:

8:43 a.m.: "KHAQQ to Itasca we are on the line 157 337. We will repeat message. We will repeat this on 6210 kilocycles. Wait."

About a minute later, Amelia radioed again:

"We are running on line north and south."

Her voice, according to those who heard it, was hurried, frantic, desperate. "I'm telling you," said the *Itasca's* chief radioman, "it sounded as if she would have broken out in a scream . . . She was just about ready to break into tears and go into hysterics."

According to official records, it was her last message.

Opposite Amelia arriving in Lae, her last stop before disappearing en route to Howland Island

7
AMELIA'S WAKE

For two hours, there was utter silence. *Itasca* received no further radio transmissions from Amelia, and by 10:15 a.m., the cutter's commander notified headquarters that she was missing, position unknown. Twenty-five minutes later, he ordered the *Itasca* to get underway and begin a search, realizing that if she and Noonan were down in the shark-infested, equatorial Pacific, they would need immediate rescue. But where to look? Amelia had stated her line of position, but she could be anywhere, north or south, along that line.

The cutter started steaming northwest of the island, perhaps based on a psychic tip from Jackie Cochran. G. P., desperate for clues after learning that Amelia was missing, had contacted Jackie and asked her to use her sixth sense to locate Amelia. She told him she had a clear vision in her mind's eye: "Amelia out of fuel . . . landed in the ocean northwest of Howland and not too far away. The plane is floating. Amelia is not hurt, but Fred Noonan bumped against the bulkhead during the water landing and is unconscious with an injured head. There is an American boat called the *Itasca* in the vicinity and also a Japanese fishing boat." Jackie gave G. P. an exact position, which he telegraphed to the *Itasca*, but the cutter found nothing when it searched the area.

G. P. also quickly cabled the chief of naval operations, Admiral William Leahy, to request help.

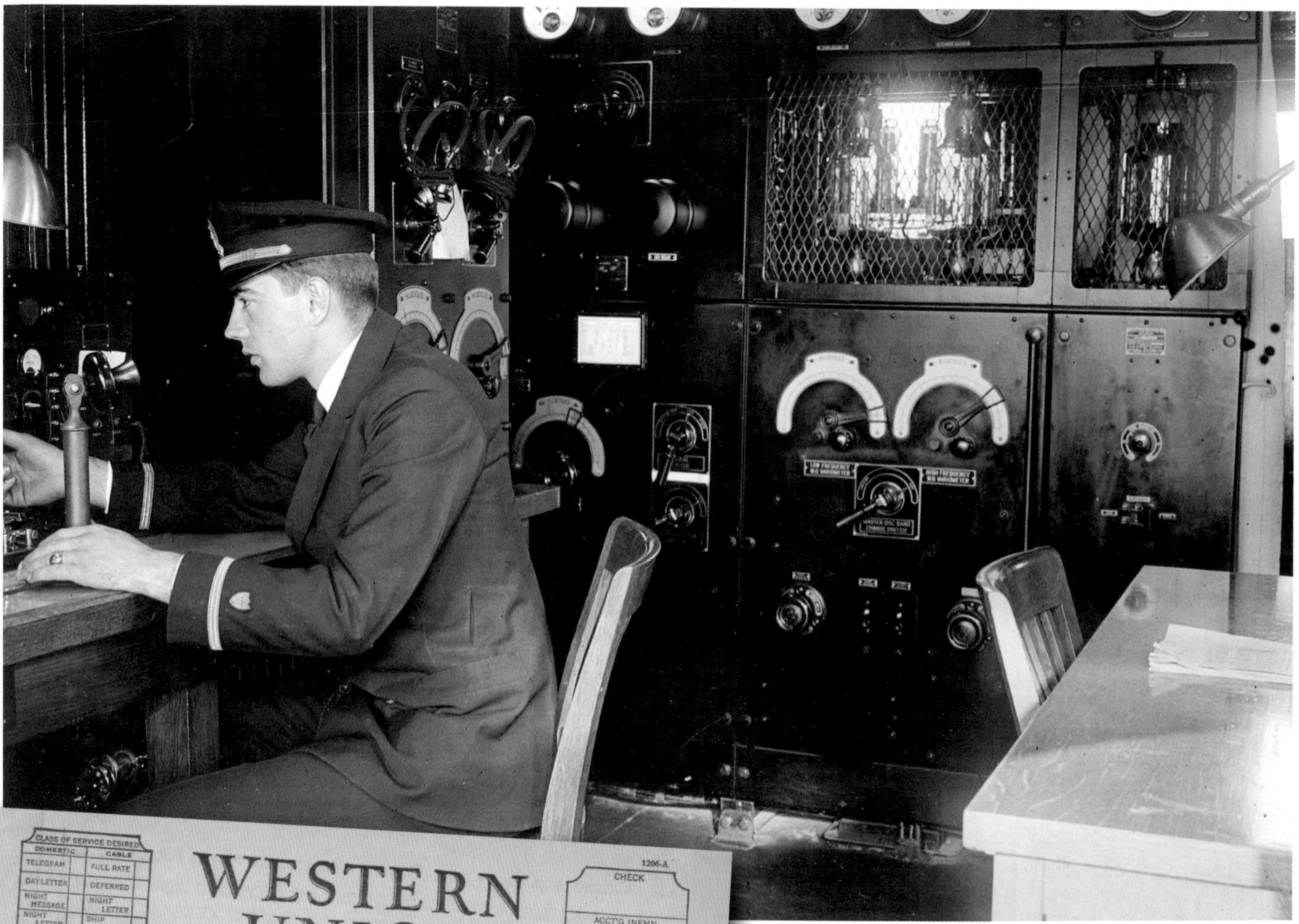

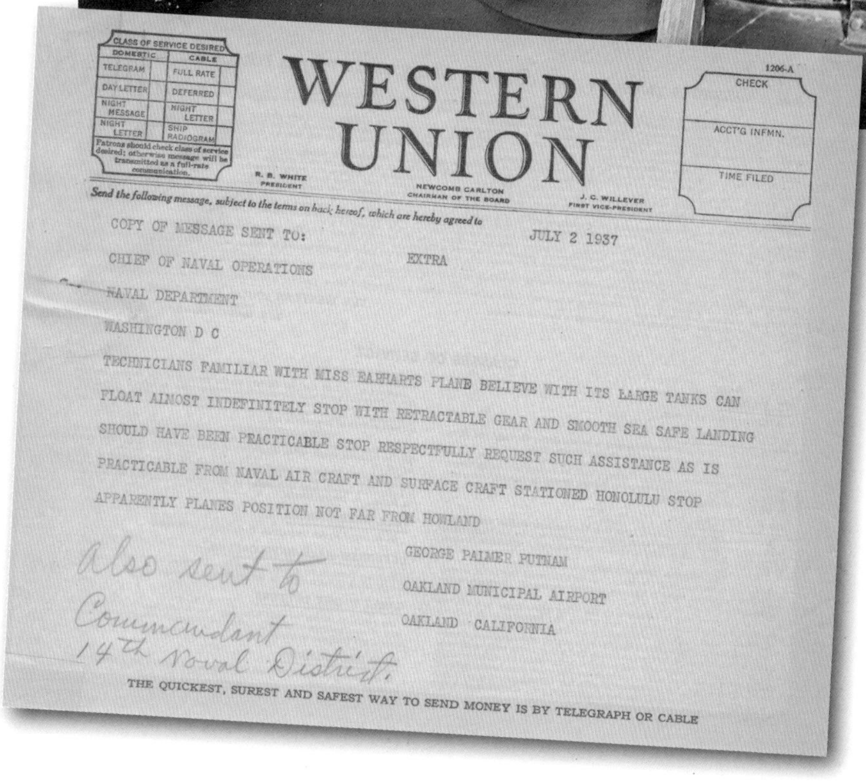

CLASS OF SERVICE DESIRED

DOMESTIC		CABLE	
TELEGRAM		FULL RATE	
DAY LETTER		DEFERRED	
NIGHT MESSAGE		NIGHT LETTER	
NIGHT LETTER		SHIP RADIOGRAM	

Patrons should check class of service desired; otherwise message will be transmitted as a full-rate communication.

WESTERN UNION

1206-A

CHECK

ACCT'G INFMN.

TIME FILED

R. B. WHITE PRESIDENT — NEWCOMB CARLTON CHAIRMAN OF THE BOARD — J. C. WILLEVER FIRST VICE-PRESIDENT

Send the following message, subject to the terms on back hereof, which are hereby agreed to

COPY OF MESSAGE SENT TO: JULY 2 1937

CHIEF OF NAVAL OPERATIONS EXTRA

NAVAL DEPARTMENT

WASHINGTON D C

TECHNICIANS FAMILIAR WITH MISS EARHARTS PLANE BELIEVE WITH ITS LARGE TANKS CAN FLOAT ALMOST INDEFINITELY STOP WITH RETRACTABLE GEAR AND SMOOTH SEA SAFE LANDING SHOULD HAVE BEEN PRACTICABLE STOP RESPECTFULLY REQUEST SUCH ASSISTANCE AS IS PRACTICABLE FROM NAVAL AIR CRAFT AND SURFACE CRAFT STATIONED HONOLULU STOP APPARENTLY PLANES POSITION NOT FAR FROM HOWLAND

GEORGE PALMER PUTNAM

OAKLAND MUNICIPAL AIRPORT

OAKLAND CALIFORNIA

Also sent to Commandant 14th Naval District.

THE QUICKEST, SUREST AND SAFEST WAY TO SEND MONEY IS BY TELEGRAPH OR CABLE

Naval assistance, however, was already mobilizing. Roosevelt instructed officials to do everything possible to locate Amelia, and Leahy had advised Admiral Orin G. Murfin, based at Hawaii's Pearl Harbor naval base, to "use in any practicable way the forces under his command to aid in the search."

An aerial hunt would be the most efficient way to comb such a wide swath of ocean, so Murfin decided to deploy the USS *Colorado*, a fast battleship carrying a thousand men and three float planes that were launched by catapult. The *Colorado*, however, was in no position to get underway. It had just pulled into port in Honolulu, and its crew, mostly young college trainees, were out on the town on

for Amelia and Noonan. The thirty-three-thousand-ton *Lexington*, with its squadron of sixty-two planes, had just docked in Santa Barbara, California, where its men had also scattered on holiday liberty. The next day, on July 4, the *Lexington*, with an escort of four destroyers, headed across the Pacific for Honolulu, where it would take on more fuel and supplies before starting the long haul to Howland.

On July 3, Jackie had telephoned G. P. to tell him she was sure that the Electra was still floating in the ocean north of the island and drifting east. The next day, however, she phoned him again to tell him that it was too late; Amelia was gone. By then, however, G. P., exhausted and haggard, was grasping for answers in mysterious messages that others were starting to receive. Faint radio signals were giving him hope that Amelia might have landed her plane on a coral reef. Water, he knew, would disable the Electra's radio batteries, located under a wing, so Amelia wouldn't be able to operate the system if she were down in the ocean. If she set down on land, however, she might have been able to get the radio working for a period of time. Beginning on July 3, radio operators in locations as far-flung as Cincinnati, Wyoming, Seattle, San Francisco, Hawaii, and the South Pacific

Fourth of July leave. The ship also needed refueling, and its planes, disassembled for maintenance, had to be put back together and made ready to fly.

A day later, on July 3, the battleship steamed out of port from Pearl Harbor, heading for Howland. The same day, the navy's fastest aircraft carrier, the *Lexington*, was also drafted to search

Page 179 The Coast Guard cutter *Itasca*, in position off Howland, reported Amelia missing on July 2.

Opposite, top The *Itasca's* radio room resembled that of its sister ship, the *Chelan*, pictured here in the mid-1930s.

Opposite, bottom G. P. wired the chief of naval operations for help after learning that Amelia had disappeared.

Left, above The battleship *Colorado* was ordered to join the search on July 3 but didn't reach Howland Island until July 7.

Left, below The navy's fastest aircraft carrier, the *Lexington*, set out from the West Coast on July 4, but it didn't arrive at Howland until July 12.

```
N. Eng. 387        U. S. NAVAL COMMUNICATION SERVICE
                                                     SRS
Received at 0735.
                                       5 JULY 1937.
FROM:   NAVY RADIO SAMOA
TO:     COAST GUARD HONOLULU


1904   0700 TO 0704 HEARD FOUR SERIES OF DASHES FROM 0714 TO 0716 HEARD
FOUR SERIES OF DASHES FROM 0727 TO 0731 HEARD EIGHT SERIES OF DASHES
FOUR OF WHICH WERE VERY STRONG VOICE INDICATED BUT NOT DISTINGUISHABLE
ALL on 3105 KCS 2045.
* * * * * * * * * * * * *
```

WESTERN UNION

```
STRAIGHT WIRE           JULY 5  1937

DAVID BINNEY PUTNAM
FORT PIERCE FLORIDA

THANKS DEAR BOY IT HELPS THERES PLENTY HOPE YET LOVE

            DAD
```

THE QUICKEST, SUREST AND SAFEST WAY TO SEND MONEY IS BY TELEGRAPH OR CABLE

Above Reports of faint radio transmissions, possibly from Amelia

Right Telegram from G. P. reassuring his son David after her disappearance

"There's plenty hope yet," G. P. believed. Meanwhile, "confidential" sources—other clairvoyants he was consulting—told him Amelia was in the water, drifting in a rubber raft hundreds of miles to the northwest of Howland. The Electra, G. P. believed, carried an inflatable life raft that was stocked with provisions. If Amelia did land in the water, she might have a chance of making it into the raft and surviving for days. Search efforts around Howland, however, yielded no clues. By July 7, the *Itasca*, joined by a slow-moving navy minesweeper, the *Swan*, had been combing the seas west, north, and east around Howland Island but had turned up no trace of the Electra or the missing flyers. That afternoon, the *Colorado* finally arrived, four days after leaving Hawaii, and sent off its planes to scan the islands, shoals, reefs, and waters hundreds of miles around Howland.

They were zeroing in on the Phoenix Group, islands two hundred eighty miles to the southeast, since static-filled radio signals, perhaps from Amelia, seemed to be originating from the island area. The *Colorado*, however, searched nearly thirty-nine thousand square miles of the region and spotted only an old shipwreck and abandoned guano works, along with signs of "recent habitation," but no human beings. By July 11, nine days after the Electra had disappeared, the *Colorado's* crew gave up all hope of finding Amelia and Noonan. The next day, on July 12, the *Lexington* finally arrived, and the carrier's planes launched a last-ditch aerial hunt, plotting every square mile of sea and reef in the area around Howland. The *Itasca* and *Swan*, meanwhile, were shifting their search to the Gilbert Islands, six hundred miles

were picking up a faint woman's voice repeating the code letters "KHAQQ, SOS, KHAQQ, SOS." At G. P.'s request, radio station KGU in Honolulu started broadcasting special hourly messages for Amelia—"AE. SOS. Land or water? North or south?"—instructing her to "respond with four long dashes if you hear us." On July 5, operators distinctly heard four dashes immediately after the broadcast instructions. Pan American and *Itasca* radio operators also picked up three dashes after asking Amelia to transmit those signals if she was on land.

to the west of Howland, where more telepathic reports of an "intimate nature," G. P. informed Murfin and Leahy, suggested that Amelia might have drifted in a lifeboat or the floating plane. He was receiving hundreds of strange, often conflicting psychic messages about her location from spiritualists and ordinary people in every state and fifteen countries, and he was determined to follow up every earthly and other-worldly possibility.

she said, "it was worth the cost . . . I only hope she went quickly and that she was not subjected to great pain." The president's concern for Amelia, however, was unabated. On July 20, his secretary suggested that he spend fifteen minutes with Gene Vidal, who had been "in very close touch with the Earhart story, talking several times a day to her husband," and had "some very interesting sidelights and some speculations, which are probably

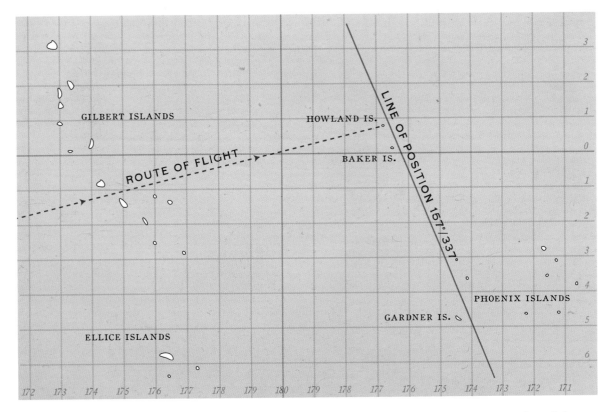

Amelia's route and the line of position she was following when she disappeared

Finally, at sunset on July 18, sixteen days after Amelia and Noonan disappeared, the United States Navy officially gave up the search. The 250,000-square-mile hunt, in every direction around Howland, was the largest sea rescue ever attempted for a missing flyer, involving four thousand men and nearly seventy American fighting planes. Eleanor Roosevelt, resigned to Amelia's loss, felt sure, she told the press, that her friend's last words had been "I have no regrets"; to Amelia,

true, as to what happened." Gene, in fact, did meet with President Roosevelt on July 30 and asked for U.S. government help in pressing the British to search their territory in the Gilbert Islands. Roosevelt must have supported the plan, and Gene and G. P.—based on "astonishingly" corroborated psychic reports—asked the State Department to urge British authorities to search the Gilbert Islands for an uncharted reef. The State Department complied with the request; on August 31, however,

YOUNGSTOWN OPENS CALUMET STEEL PLANTS TO 7000

HELEN MOODY AT TAHOE; MAPS NEV. DIVORCE

The World Remembers • Amelia's Exploits • As 'Last Hope' Hunt Starts

LAST OF STRIKE BOUND MILLS TO OPEN

By United Press

RENO, July 13.—Helen Wills Moody, who for years was an international tennis champion, was settled in a rustic cottage on the shores of Lake Tahoe today to establish the six weeks residence required for a divorce in Nevada.

She already had conferred with Robert M. Price, prominent Reno divorce lawyer, and she admitted to reporters, after much cautious word bartering, that it was her intention to divorce Frederick S. Moody jr., oil executive and member of a prominent San Francisco family.

MOODY VACATIONS

They were married Dec. 23, 1929, after a romance that started on the French Riviera.

At the Moody home in San Francisco it was reported that he was on a two-weeks hunting vacation in northern California. It was his sister-in-law, Mrs. Corbitt Moody, of San Mateo, who first tipped off the news that the "Poker Face" of the tennis court expected to divorce her husband.

"Of course she went to Nevada to get a divorce," Mrs. Corbitt Moody said.

Armed with this statement, reporters forced the reluctant admission from the tennis star that she visited Attorney Price. That she had separated from her husband and that "once my mind is made up I see no reason for prolonging anything."

GROUNDS UNDECIDED

She was asked what grounds she would charge in a divorce suit, and answered that she supposed "anything like that would be up to Mr. Price."

Mrs. Moody arrived yesterday at fashionable Glenbrook with her Sealyham dog and enough baggage for a prolonged visit.

A possible rift between the Moodys long had been rumored, but was denied consistently by Mrs. Moody until her arrival here.

She laughed when asked if there was another romance in her life.

"People get so many funny ideas," she said.

TWO STABBED IN DOWNTOWN CHASE

After a wild chase during which two men suffered severe stab wounds, Joe Martinez, 14-year-old burglary suspect, today was finally captured by a group of irate citizens from whom officers were forced to rescue him.

Martinez, according to police reports, entered a clothing store at 228 South Main street, grabbed seven shirts off the counter and ran out into the street. Ralph Van Zant, 22, of 1220½ North Edgemont, clerk in the store, ran after him and using football tactics, tackled him, but was severely stabbed in the abdomen when Martinez drew a pocket knife with a seven-inch blade, police said.

Seeing the fallen clerk, a citizen, Harry F. Robinson, 35, 236 East Sixtieth street, took after the fleeing boy, but was severely stopped in the head when he attempted to grab him, the report read. Martinez then was caught by a group of angered citizens who knocked him down and kicked him just as police arrived upon the scene, it was reported.

By Associated Press

EAST CHICAGO, Ind., July 13.—Youngstown Sheet and Tube Co. threw open the gates of its Calumet District steel plants today for all of its 7000 employes who desired to return to work.

The reopening, after a shutdown of 46 days, signalized resumption of operations by the last of the strike-bound plants in northern Indiana.

Leaders of the Steel Workers Organizing Committee, which called the strike and their followers hailed the reopening as a Committee for Industrial Organization victory, but their claims were disputed by the company and the Association of Steel Employes, an independent union.

Governor M. Clifford Townsend of Indiana declared the company and the S. W. O. C. had come to terms. Vice President J. C. Argetsinger of Sheet and Tube said the company had made no agreement and had granted concessions to no one.

The lack of understanding was reflected in the actions of strikers. On three occasions yesterday pickets massed about the firm's Indiana Harbor plant only to be called away by their leaders.

'SATISFACTORY POLICY'

Governor Townsend said the company voluntarily submitted a satisfactory labor policy to the S. W. O. C. and that it therefore was morally obligated to abide by that policy.

The company announced it would post signs at its plants stating the reopening was the result of demands by employes and not through any pressure by or agreement with the Steel Workers Organization Committee.

Van A. Bittner, Steel Workers Organization Committee regional director, announced the Committee for Industrial Organization had won a victory "through the truce arranged by Governor Townsend." His announcement was the signal for "victory" celebrations.

At the same time H. O. Brown, president of the Association of Steel Employes, declared it was a victory for that organization.

Rivalry between the two labor organizations was blamed by police for a fight yesterday in front of the independent union's headquarters. One man was severely beaten. Three men were arrested.

(For other strike news see Page A-8.)

HOUSE OVERRIDES FARM LOAN VETO

By Associated Press

WASHINGTON, July 13.—The House overrode today President Roosevelt's veto of a bill to continue low interest rates on farm loans for two more years.

With a two-thirds majority of those voting required to override, Speaker Bankhead announced the vote was 260 to 97.

The Senate has yet to act.

House action came after an hour's debate during which the chief executive's objections to the legislation were criticized and defended.

It was the second time this session the House had overridden a veto. Several who a year ago it joined the Senate in overriding legislation extending the time in which World War veterans might convert term life insurance policies.

As navy planes today launch the "last hope" hunt in the South Pacific for Amelia Earhart the world recalls her exploits. She is shown after she spanned the Atlantic in 1932, the first woman to do it alone.

After her triumphal return from Europe Miss Earhart won new laurels in aviation. She's shown after setting a new women's cross-country record from Los Angeles to New York in July, 1932.

Amelia began her flying career in Glendale in 1918 when she pawned her jewels and furs to buy her first plane. She's shown in her first flying togs.

Because she looks so much like Charles Lindbergh and her record has paralleled his, she is often called "Lady Lindy." She is shown at left, Lindbergh at right.

The Pacific ocean had claimed the lives of 10 intrepid fliers when Miss Earhart determined to be the first woman to make the Hawaii-Oakland flight. She is shown being greeted after completing the hop in 1935.

Amelia is pictured with her husband, George Palmer Putnam, wealthy publisher, whom she wed in 1931. Now he is in Los Angeles closely following the flight of navy planes seeking her in South Pacific wastes.

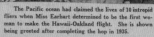

After her first Pacific flight, Miss Earhart won new fame by being the first woman to fly from Los Angeles to Mexico City. She's shown in a tumultuous reception in Mexico City. On this flight she was blinded by an insect in her eye. Then she set a record in her solo flight from Mexico City to New York.

Out of her flying togs Miss Earhart always was as charmingly feminine as any woman dreams to be. She is shown above in a lacy evening gown. Between flights she rested in her home near Los Angeles.

Misfortunes have never bothered Miss Earhart. She's shown with Fred Noonan, navigator now lost with her, on the wing of her $75,000 "flying laboratory" after it crashed in Hawaii. She had it repaired and started her world flight anew. Known as the "smiling aviatrix," she sought to glorify aviation.

British officials reported that the area had indeed been searched, with no trace of any uncharted reefs or a downed airplane.

G. P., however, couldn't rest until he had followed every possible lead, and he refused to admit that Amelia was dead without conclusive

By mid-September, G. P. was still receiving packages, photographs, and letters that Amelia had posted to him from around the world. There was perhaps only "one chance in a thousand," he now admitted, that she was still alive, and the Coast Guard had stated that radio signals thought to be distress messages from Amelia were either fakes or transmissions from other sources. G. P., however, remained unconvinced and was still looking for answers. He considered sending out his own expedition to hunt for her, a costly proposition, while other investigators took up the challenge. In October a private schooner—outfitted with diving and movie equipment—was preparing to sail for the South Pacific to search for Amelia. Other private expeditions combed the Phoenix,

July 23,1937 a.m.

Secretary of the Navy.
Washington,

Please accept my gratitude for generous and efficient conduct of Amelia Earhart search stop respectfully request your good offices in obtaining cooperation of british and Japanese in continueing search especially regarding ellice and Marshall islands ocean island and area northeast of same stop also if possible request some examination of islands northerly and northwesterly of pago pago stop seek leave no try undone looking toward securing information stop whatever it may be possible to do will be sincerely appreciated.

G.P.Putnam,

To; Roper

Unquote for your confidential information extraordinary evidence seems to exist indicating castaways still living though of such strange nature cannot be officially or bublicaly considered my thanks to you.

Opposite A page from the *Los Angeles Evening Herald and Express* remembering Amelia's life

Left Typescript copy of a telegram G. P. sent to the Secretary of the Navy citing "extraordinary evidence" of a "strange nature" from pyschic sources

Below Envelope that Amelia mailed herself four days before she vanished

evidence. In late July he had offered a reward of $2,000 for information that would solve the mystery of her disappearance. Days later, a man came forward in possession of Amelia's brown and white scarf, claiming the reward money and stating that she had been rescued by smugglers and was still alive. The scarf was, in fact, really Amelia's—it had blown off her neck into his hands when he watched her climb out of her cockpit three years earlier— but the story was a hoax, and the scammer was arrested.

Gilbert, and Marshall Islands, but none of them found any clues to the mystery of her disappearance.

Still, the hunts gave Amelia's mother, Amy, reason for hope. Neta Snook, Amelia's first flying teacher, visited Amy months after Amelia vanished. When she walked through the front door, she saw on the wall a life-sized portrait of Amelia as a ten-year-old girl, wearing a white dress with a big white bow in her blond hair. "Mother Earhart," Neta remembered, "welcomed me with open arms" and talked about the private searches that were going on, long after the government had given up. Amy was "greatly disturbed," Neta recalled, but she seemed "full of hope." For two years, in fact, Amy, according to Muriel, kept "a suitcase packed with a few light clothes, cold cream for sunburn, and scissors to cut her hair," in case Amelia was suddenly found on a tropical island.

Amy Earhart hoped that private expeditions to the South Pacific would find her daughter.

As the months wore on, G. P. finally reconciled himself to Amelia's loss, and in December 1938, he filed her will for probate. Amelia's estate, valued at more than $10,000, included property, royalties, bonds, and accounts receivable. A month later, on January 6, 1939, a Los Angeles superior court judge legally declared her dead.

Amelia was officially gone, but she was hardly forgotten, and the legends and speculation about her disappearance were only beginning. G. P., always a publicist, was fanning the flames. In 1937, soon after Amelia disappeared, he submitted a story to RKO Pictures titled "Lady with Wings: The Life Story of My Wife, Amelia Earhart." The studio passed on the project, noting it was "staying away from all airplane pictures in the immediate future," but G. P., with his Hollywood contacts, kept pitching the film. In 1939, he contracted with the producer of the movie *Pygmalion* to collaborate on a screenplay about Amelia's life, which was never produced.

In 1943, however—two years after Japan attacked Pearl Harbor—a fictional story loosely based on Amelia's life made it to the big screen. Titled *Flight for Freedom* and produced for RKO under studio head Floyd Odlum, Jackie Cochran's husband, the movie starred Rosalind Russell as an eye-catching aviator named Tonie Carter. The movie follows Carter's career fighting bias against women pilots and building a record-setting reputation as a "Lady Lindy." In the end, Carter takes off on a secret government mission to aid the U.S. effort against Japan, then deliberately crashes her plane into the Pacific so the navy can launch a search effort and investigate suspected Japanese installations. The movie played to audiences all over America, as well as thousands of U.S. troops stationed in the Pacific, igniting rampant speculation that Amelia had, in fact, been on a secret government mission when she disappeared. Eleanor and Franklin Roosevelt, however, denied the rumors. Gore Vidal asked Eleanor, years later, if she had discovered anything about an undercover mission, and she said she hadn't. "More to the point," Vidal wrote, "since Mrs. Roosevelt had been devoted to Amelia, if there *had* been a secret mission," she would have "revealed it after the war and demanded all sorts of posthumous recognition for her friend." Eleanor, however, "was certain that there had been no spy mission," although she did think "there *was* something fishy about the whole business."

Others subscribed to the notion that Amelia had been captured and held prisoner by the Japanese—a theory that Amy eventually believed and promoted after the war. In 1949, she made a public statement that Amelia had "died in Japan" on a mission for the U.S. government. Amy explained that she had "kept quiet" about this opinion but believed that Amelia had landed on a tiny atoll, where she had been picked up by a Japanese fishing boat. Amelia, she continued, had then been taken to the Marshall Islands and finally Japan, where "she met with an accident," Amy asserted— "an 'arranged' accident that ended her life."

Although separate investigations by United Press and U.S. Army Intelligence found no evidence that Amelia had been captured by the Japanese, the theory was revived in the 1960s by Fred Goerner, a reporter for CBS radio in San Francisco. Goerner was intrigued by the story of a northern California woman, Josephine Blanco Akiyama, who claimed

The 1943 movie *Flight for Freedom*— a fictional account based loosely on Amelia's life—ignited rumors that she had been on a secret spy mission for the U.S. government.

to have seen Amelia and Noonan on Saipan, an island in the Marianas, in 1937. Saipan was fifteen hundred miles north of Lae, New Guinea, dramatically far afield from Amelia's reported route. Nevertheless, Goerner made four trips to Saipan—funded by CBS, the Associated Press, Scripps newspapers, and the *San Mateo Times*—and interviewed individuals who told him that they had seen the flyers. Goerner theorized that Amelia and Noonan were on an unofficial espionage mission for the U.S. government to observe airfields and Japanese fleet facilities on the island of Truk in the central Carolines. After they finished their reconnaissance work, the flyers headed for Howland but ran into weather problems; then,

low on fuel, they made a landing in Japanese territory at Mili Atoll in the southern Marshalls. Soon after, Goerner believed, they were picked up by a Japanese fishing boat and transported to Saipan, where they were imprisoned and possibly tortured and executed. Goerner's book, published in 1966, was a national bestseller for half a year, and all of a sudden, Amelia Earhart conspiracy theories were back in vogue.

In 1970, two former air force officers, Joseph Klass and Joseph Gervais, came up with a new twist to the espionage story. They published a book claiming that Amelia had been captured by the Japanese on a secret spy mission for FDR and imprisoned in Tokyo's Imperial Palace. Then, in

1945, they asserted, she was secretly released and resumed her life under a new name, Mrs. Irene Bolam, a widow who was then living in a New Jersey retirement community. Mrs. Bolam, outraged, protested that she had been living in Mineola, New York, during the years when Amelia was supposedly imprisoned. She dismissed the claims as "utter nonsense" and a "poorly documented hoax," and the publisher withdrew the book from the market. Still, as late as 1994, the spy theory was still being promulgated by another author, Randall Brink. He argued that Amelia's Electra was specially equipped to photograph Japanese military installations in the Pacific and that she was forced down, captured by the Japanese, and taken to Saipan as a prisoner of war, ending up as one of the Japanese broadcasting propagandists known as "Tokyo Rose." G. P., however, had listened carefully to many broadcasts of Tokyo Rose during World War II, and none of them, he determined, were made by Amelia.

Despite the continuing popularity of Japanese-capture theories, no physical or documentary evidence was ever found to support them.

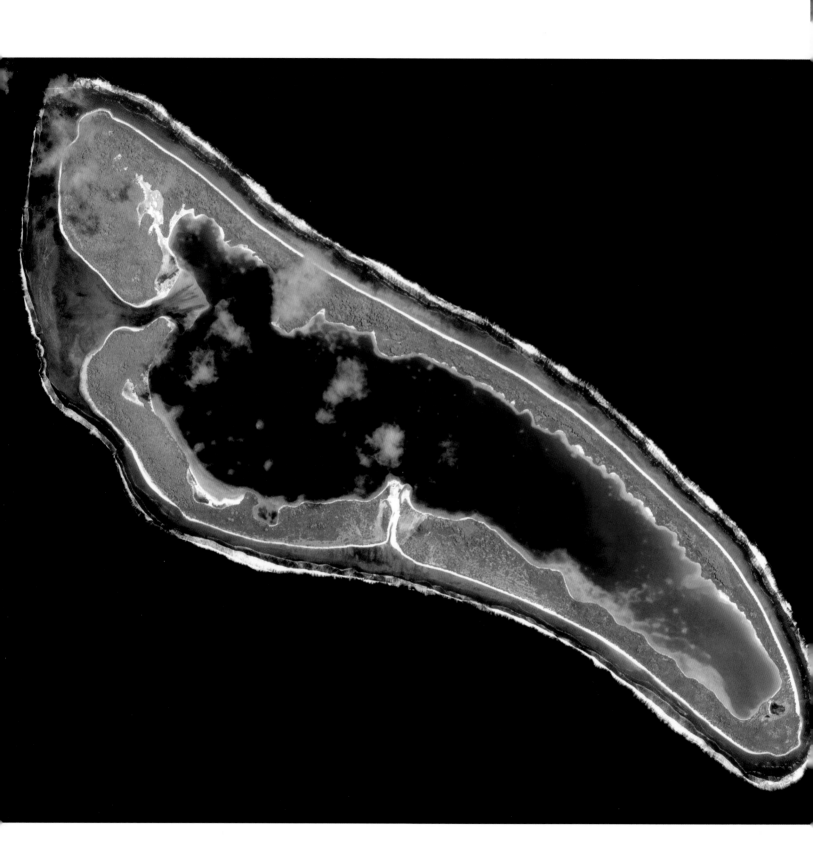

The Saipan story, in particular, was refuted in the 1980s by a Japanese journalist named Fukiko Aoki. Aoki interviewed surviving individuals whom Goerner had questioned in the 1960s. In her book, published in Japanese, she argued that Goerner had essentially led his witnesses, who were happy to go along with the story he was suggesting because they liked the attention and wanted to make a good impression.

By the 1990s, some investigators were turning to another hypothesis: that Amelia had landed her Electra on Gardner Island (now called Nikumaroro) in the Phoenix Group southeast of Howland, where G. P. and the U.S. Navy, for a time, believed that she had ended up. Members of The International Group for Historic Aircraft

Recovery (TIGHAR)—founded in 1985 by Richard E. Gillespie, a former aviation accident insurance investigator, and his wife, Pat Thrasher—have conducted nine archaeological expeditions to Nikumaroro, most recently in 2007.

Over the past twenty years, TIGHAR's historians, scientists, professional pilots, engineers, and forensic experts have studied all aspects of Amelia's last flight and disappearance. The team's radio propagation specialists, in particular, have analyzed radio distress calls after her last officially recorded message, concluding that Amelia and Noonan were, indeed, sending transmissions from the Phoenix Group for days after they vanished. "While some of the signals were transparent hoaxes," Gillespie concedes, "nearly a hundred

Opposite and left Some investigators believe that Amelia landed on uninhabited Gardner Island, now called Nikumaroro.

of the transmissions suggest that Amelia was on an island in the Phoenix Group calling for help. If not," he argues, "there were hoaxers in that area who were able to transmit on her frequency, mimic her voice, knew a lot about her, and knew that she was going to vanish so they could position themselves."

According to a theory that Gillespie and TIGHAR have been piecing together over the years, Amelia and Noonan were stranded as castaways on dry, desolate, uninhabited Gardner Island until

their deaths. Gillespie believes that after about twenty hours of flying, with three to four hours of fuel remaining and no visual or two-way radio contact with the *Itasca* or Howland Island, the flyers decided to head southeast along their line of position. In that direction, the Pacific is dotted with a few coral islands, compared to the empty stretch of ocean to the northwest. By 10:45 a.m., he says, they would have seen Gardner Island, with its big turquoise lagoon. At low tide, the reef on the west end of the island would have looked smooth and dry,

thundered over the island, Amelia and Noonan heard the engines but couldn't make it back to the beach in time to be spotted. Although the searchers saw signs of recent habitation, they didn't observe any human beings. If part of the Electra had been visible through the crashing surf, the pilots might have thought it was part of the shipwreck lying nearby on the coral reef.

Nine days later, when the search ended, Amelia and Noonan found themselves marooned on the desert island, trying to survive. There was no source of fresh water on the atoll, but they could have managed for a time, Gillespie theorizes, on birds, small fish, and clams, as well as provisions that had been left behind by survivors of the *Norwich City.* Eventually, Gillespie believes, the two of them perished from thirst, food poisoning, injury, or infection. The Electra, TIGHAR theorizes, was broken up by pounding surf; when the island was inhabited for a brief time, from 1938 to 1963, the residents probably scavenged any remaining debris.

and Amelia, he believes, landed the plane there, near the wreck of an old freighter, the *Norwich City,* that had run aground on the island in 1929. Amelia and Noonan, Gillespie asserts, ran the engine to keep the plane's generator and radio batteries charged and sent distress signals at night, when transmissions are stronger, which were heard by the navy, the Coast Guard, and short-wave radio operators over the next three days.

After about a week, however, rising tides and high surf on the coral reef would have forced Amelia and Noonan to abandon the Electra and seek shelter from the searing sun in dense inland brush. On July 9, when the *Colorado's* planes

TIGHAR's theory, Gillespie says, is based on historic, archaeological, and forensic evidence. In October 1937, three months after Amelia and Noonan disappeared, a small British expedition to Gardner Island noted unexplained "signs of previous habitation" along the shore, "like someone had bivouaced for the night." Then, in 1940, a member of a native work party found a human skull. That September, a British colonial administrator, Gerald Gallagher, came to live on the atoll. At the site where the worker came across the skull, Gallagher discovered a campsite and some

Opposite A freighter, the *Norwich City,* ran aground on Gardner Island in 1929.

Left Dense brush and trees covered the coral atoll in 1937.

In 2006, deep-sea recovery expert David Jourdan led his second expedition, aboard the research vessel *Davidson*, to hunt for the Electra at the bottom of the Pacific, seventeen thousand feet below the surface.

scattered bones, along with evidence of a campfire, bird and turtle remains, and a sextant box marked with a series of numbers. Near the bones, he discovered remains of a woman's and a man's shoe and "corks with brass chains," perhaps from small casks that came from the *Norwich City* stores. Extensive British government records, according to TIGHAR, confirm and document the 1940 discoveries on Gardner Island.

Since Gallagher suspected the remains could be Amelia's, he shipped the bones and artifacts to British headquarters in Fiji for "strictly secret" examination. In April 1941, a colonial doctor analyzed the bones and concluded that they probably came from a muscular middle-aged male of

European descent. Although the bones themselves have since disappeared, TIGHAR researchers discovered the doctor's measurements and notes. In 1998, forensic investigators reanalyzed them and found them consistent with a white female of northern European extraction who was about five feet seven inches tall.

In 2001, a TIGHAR expedition to the island located the site Gallagher reported, cleared the vegetation, and found evidence of habitation. A more detailed examination of the site in 2007 found additional artifacts, including a piece of a woman's powder compact, a civilian zipper, and the bottom of a broken hand-lotion bottle, all manufactured in the U.S. and dating from the mid-1930s. According to a forensic anthropologist at the University of Alabama, the fire area, littered with more than a thousand bones and shells, is consistent with a campsite of western castaways who were subsisting on anything that they could find to eat. TIGHAR investigators also determined that the series of numbers on the sextant box found with the bones in 1940 matches those on a type of sextant that Noonan was known to have carried.

In the absence of conclusive proof—a DNA sample or an airplane part marked with a serial number—all of TIGHAR's evidence to date has been circumstantial. Nevertheless, Gillespie says,

TIGHAR's researchers are convinced of the theory "based on a preponderance of historical and physical evidence and the credibility of the post-loss calls. We think the record establishes," he argues, "that Amelia, Noonan, and the Electra didn't go down at sea."

Other investigators disagree. Elgen Long—a navy radio operator, navigator, and pilot who has been studying Amelia's disappearance for thirty years—is the leading proponent of the competing "crashed and sank" theory. He argues that Amelia and Noonan ran out of gas and ditched in the Pacific, within fifty-two miles of Howland Island.

The *Davidson* towed a side-scan sonar system to acoustically image large swaths of the ocean bottom.

Within a short time, he believes, the Electra filled with water and sank seventeen thousand feet to the bottom of the ocean.

David Jourdan, a former navy submariner and ocean engineer specializing in deep-sea recoveries, has been using this theory to hunt for the Electra over the last decade. Since purchasing Long's research materials in the late 1990s, Jourdan has organized two deep-ocean sonar searches, in 2002 and 2006, in the area of the Pacific around Howland Island. Long's investigation suggests that the Electra sank in a six-thousand-square-mile area north and west of the island. On the deep ocean floor, where there's little light, oxygen, or silt, Jourdan believes that the Electra would be well preserved. To narrow the search area, he relied on fuel and radio analyses, identifying a likely grid of around twelve hundred square nautical miles, about the size of Rhode Island.

In 2002, Jourdan's company, Nauticos, mapped six hundred square miles of this probable area by slowly towing a sonar device back and forth over wide swaths of the ocean, acoustically mapping the sea floor and any debris. Four years later, Jourdan returned to the site, mapping another six hundred square miles. It's a difficult and expensive project. The search area is so remote that it takes a week to travel there by ship from Hawaii, and the cost of a single mission is around $2 million.

Although Jourdan hasn't yet located the Electra, he is confident that he eventually will. Over the years, his team has discovered the deep-water wreck of a World War II Japanese submarine, the *I-52,* on the ocean bottom at seventeen thousand feet, as well as the *Kaga,* a Japanese aircraft carrier sunk in the Battle of Midway, five hundred feet deeper. His team also found the *Dakar,* an Israeli sub that was lost in the Mediterranean in 1968, along with the deepest ancient shipwreck ever

discovered, from the third century B.C. Locating Amelia's Electra, Jourdan believes, is just a matter of time. "We still need to scan about 5 percent of the highly probable area," he says, "and I think we'll find it."

Until then, and in the absence of a "smoking gun," Amelia's disappearance is just as baffling today as it was in 1937. She was one of the most famous women in America; then she vanished abruptly, with the whole world watching. And although she was flying farther and longer than ever, she was at the end of her arc. The era of heroic "hot aeronautics," which launched her celebrity, was already closing. The dangers and distances that had drawn legends like Amelia and Lindbergh were growing routine. Days after Amelia disappeared over the Pacific, commercial planes, for the first time, flew over the Atlantic Ocean in both directions. "The future," declared a writer for the *New York Post,* "lies with the undramatic experts who bring the planes in on time, safely. The romantic whoopla artists," he added, had outstayed their welcome.

But Amelia had always been more than a publicity-seeking "aeronautical entrepreneur." She was driven less by a desire for headlines than her inner compulsion to gamble for the highest stakes. At risk was her life, which she was ready to lose, she said time and again, for the sheer thrill and the joy of doing what she wanted to do.

Opposite Amelia and her Lockheed Vega

FLYING RECORDS

1922   Sets unofficial women's altitude record of 14,000 feet

1928   First woman to fly across the Atlantic Ocean as a passenger

1930   Sets women's speed record for 100 kilometers with no load and with 500-kilogram load

Sets women's world speed record of 181.18 miles per hour over a 3-kilometer course

1931   Sets women's autogiro altitude record of 18,415 feet

1932   First woman (and second person) to fly solo across the Atlantic Ocean, in 14 hours, 56 minutes

First person to cross the Atlantic Ocean twice in an airplane

First woman to fly nonstop solo coast to coast

Sets women's transcontinental speed record (Los Angeles, California, to Newark, New Jersey), flying 2,447.8 miles in 19 hours, 5 minutes

Awarded the Army Air Corps Distinguished Flying Cross

Awarded the National Geographic Society's Gold Medal by President Herbert Hoover

1933   Breaks her previous transcontinental speed record with flying time of 17 hours, 7 minutes, 30 seconds

1935   First person to fly solo 2,408 miles across the Pacific Ocean from Honolulu, Hawaii, to Oakland, California

First civilian to fly an airplane carrying a two-way radio

First person to fly solo from Los Angeles to Mexico City, Mexico, in 13 hours, 23 minutes

First person to fly nonstop solo from Mexico City to Newark, in 14 hours, 19 minutes

1937   First person to fly from the Red Sea to India

SELECTED BIBLIOGRAPHY

UNPUBLISHED SOURCES

MANUSCRIPT COLLECTIONS AND PERSONAL PAPERS
Purdue University Archives and Special Collections
George Palmer Putnam Collection of Amelia Earhart Papers

The Schlesinger Library, Radcliffe Institute, Harvard University
Earhart, Amelia
Earhart, Amy Otis
Mabie, Janet
Denison House

PUBLISHED SOURCES

Backus, Jean L. *Letters from Amelia.* Boston: Beacon Press, 1982.

Butler, Susan. *East to the Dawn.* New York: Da Capo Press, 1999.

Chapman, Sally Putnam. *Whistled Like a Bird,* New York: Warner Books, 1997.

Cochran, Jacqueline, and Maryann Bucknum Brinley. *Jackie Cochran: An Autobiography.* New York: Bantam Books, 1987.

Cook, Blanche Wiesen. *Eleanor Roosevelt: The Defining Years.* New York: Viking Penguin, 1999.

Earhart, Amelia. *20 Hrs., 40 Min.: Our Flight in the Friendship.* Washington, D.C.: National Geographic Society, 2003.

————. *The Fun of It.* New York: Harcourt Brace Jovanovich, Inc., 1932.

————. *Last Flight.* New York: Harcourt, Brace & World, Inc., 1937.

Gillespie, Ric. *Finding Amelia.* Annapolis, MD: Naval Institute Press, 2006.

Goerner, Fred. *The Search for Amelia Earhart.* New York: Doubleday & Company, Inc., 1966.

Hardesty, Von. *Lindbergh: Flight's Enigmatic Hero.* New York: Harcourt, Inc., 2002.

King, Thomas F., Randall S. Jacobson, Karen R. Burns, Kenton Spading. *Amelia Earhart's Shoes.* Walnut Creek, CA: Alatamira Press, 2004.

Lebow, Eileen F. *Before Amelia.* Washington, D.C.: Brassey's, Inc, 2002.

Leider, Emily Wortis. *Becoming Mae West.* Cambridge, MA: Da Capo Press, 2000.

Long, Elgen M., and Marie K., *Amelia Earhart: The Mystery Solved.* New York: Simon & Schuster, 1999.

Lovell, Mary S. *The Sound of Wings.* New York: St. Martin's Press, 1989.

Lubben, Kristen, and Erin Barnett, eds. *Amelia Earhart: Image and Icon.* New York: International Center of Photography, 2007.

Morrissey, Muriel Earhart. *Courage Is the Price.* Wichita, KS: McCormick-Armstrong, 1963.

Morrissey, Muriel Earhart, and Osborne, Carol L. *Amelia, My Courageous Sister.* Santa Clara, CA: Osborne Publisher, Inc., 1987.

Nichols, Ruth. *Wings for Life.* New York: J. B. Lippincott Company, 1957.

Putnam, George Palmer. *Soaring Wings*. New York: Manor Books, 1972.

———. *Wide Margins*. New York: Harcourt, Brace and Company, 1942.

Railey, Hilton Howell. *Touch'd with Madness*. New York: Carrick & Evans, Inc., 1938.

Rich, Doris L. *Amelia Earhart: A Biography*. Washington, D.C.: Smithsonian Institution Press, 1989.

Smith, Elinor. *Aviatrix*. Thorndike, ME: Thorndike Press, 1982.

Southern, Neta Snook. *I Taught Amelia To Fly*. New York: Vantage Press, 1974.

Thaden, Louise. *High, Wide, and Frightened*. Fayetteville, AR: The University of Arkansas Press, 2004.

Vidal, Gore. *Point to Point Navigation*. New York: Vintage Books, 2006.

———. *United States: Essays 1952–1992*. New York: Random House, 1993.

PERIODICALS

American Heritage
The American Magazine
Cosmopolitan
Invention & Technology
Journal of the History of Medicine and Allied Sciences
Liberty
Popular Aviation
Provenance
Smithsonian Studies in Air and Space
Time

NEWSPAPERS

Allentown Call
Amarillo Daily News
Ann Arbor News
Auburn Citizen
Birmingham Gazette
Boston Globe
Boston Herald
Chautauquan Daily
Cheyenne Tribune
Chicago Times
Christian Science Monitor
Daily Dispatch
Daily Mining Journal
Daily Mirror
Dallas Times Herald
Dayton Daily News
Dayton Journal
Evansville Courier
Evening Star
Knoxville Journal
Lincoln State Journal
Los Angeles Examiner
Los Angeles Times
Louisville Courier
Macon Telegraph
Miami Herald
Muncie Star
New Bedford Times
New York American
New York Herald Tribune
New York Sun
New York Telegram
New York Times
Oakland Tribune
Omaha Bee-News
Philadelphia Bulletin
Prairie Farmer
Reno Gazette
Richmond Times
San Francisco Chronicle
Savannah News
Shelby Star
Sioux City Journal
South Bend News-Times
Terre Haute Star
Toronto Daily Star
Troy Times
Washington Herald
Washington Post
Women's Wear Daily
Worcester Post

INDEX

PHOTOGRAPHY CREDITS

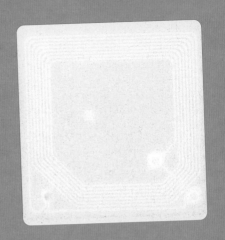

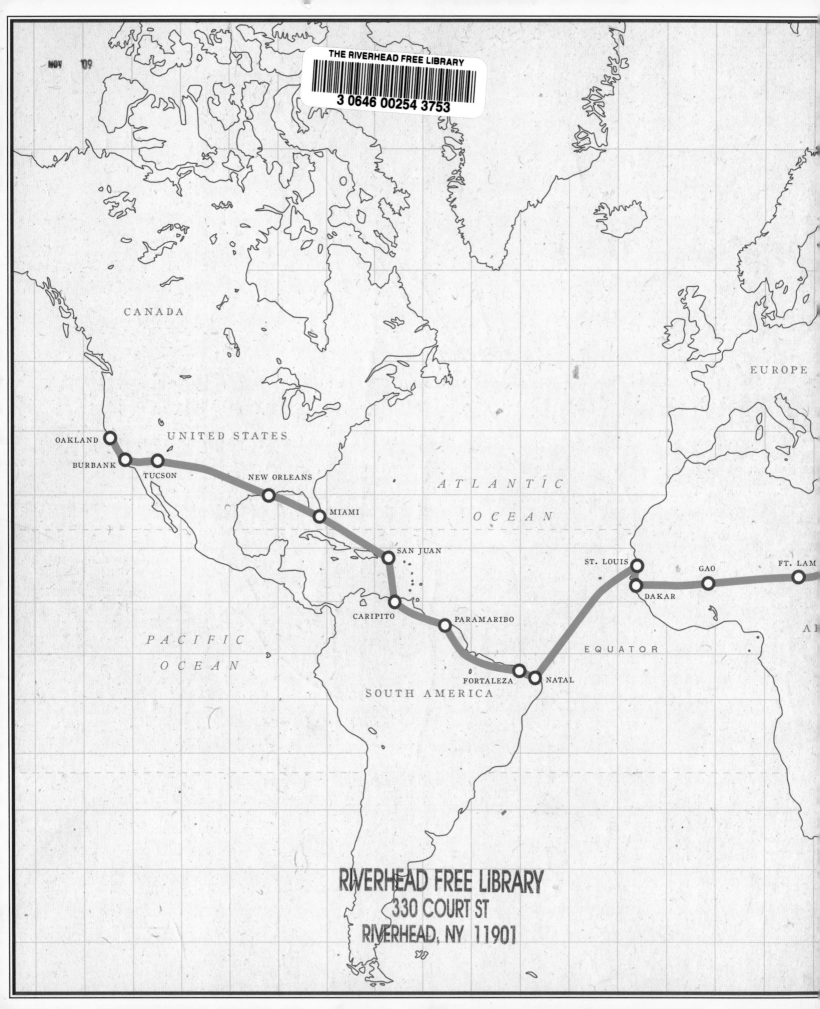

OAKLAND
BURBANK
TUCSON
NEW ORLEANS
MIAMI

UNITED STATES

CANADA

EUROPE

ATLANTIC
OCEAN

SAN JUAN

ST. LOUIS
DAKAR
GAO
FT. LAM

CARIPITO
PARAMARIBO

AF

PACIFIC
OCEAN

EQUATOR

FORTALEZA
NATAL

SOUTH AMERICA